A Study Companion on the Gospel of John

EXPOSITION, INTERPRETATION, AND COMMENTARY

Sherrill Gardner Stevens

© 2020
Published in the United States by Nurturing Faith Inc., Macon GA,
www.nurturingfaith.net.

Nurturing Faith is the book publishing arm of Good Faith Media (goodfaithmedia.org).

Library of Congress Cataloging-in-Publication Data is available.

ISBN: 978-1-63528-116-3

All rights reserved. Printed in the United States of America.

"As a member of the laity in the Christian church, I have always had trouble with the concept of just reading the latest translation of the Bible and instinctively understanding it. Therefore, I have relied on individuals such as William Barclay, N.T. Wright, and C.S. Lewis to provide the necessary historical research, contextual perspective, and translation of Hebrew and Greek words to help me better understand the Bible. Sherrill Stevens' *A Study Companion on the Gospel of John* follows in the tradition of these giants, exploring the scripture in ways that lead to a deeper understanding of the scripture and, at times, challenging readers to think beyond what they have learned previously in Sunday School or Bible study. Nearly half a century of learning and studying scripture echo in the words of Dr. Stevens as he leads readers through the Gospel of John, taking time to explain the nuances of the text while also tying in the big picture by referencing other scriptural passages. The genius of Dr. Stevens is that he does not let his intellectual analysis of the scripture overshadow the feeling of love and adoration with which he approaches his study of the life of Jesus. I am grateful that Dr. Stevens' heart of servitude has led to this compilation of his life-long study of scripture."

Lance Rogers
Mt. Sylvan United Methodist Church
Durham, North Carolina

"As a lay teacher of an adult Sunday School class, I have to 'keep on my toes.' In the beginning, I read the scripture lessons, studied it, and took notes. We had class discussions that stimulated more interest and more study. Bible dictionaries and different Bible translations came next. Then, I discovered Bible commentaries. Dr. Stevens' book on the Gospel of John is comprehensive in its scope; it is more than a commentary. The political, historical, and especially spiritual aspects of his work have resulted in some thinking and rethinking, inviting and maybe challenging us to do more Bible study—which I call a good thing!"

Pam Mentz
Black Creek Baptist Church
Mechanicsville, Virginia

"Sherrill Stevens brings many years of biblical study experience to this wonderful new commentary on the Gospel of John. It is well organized and researched, succinctly written, and promises to be helpful to clergy and laity alike."

Glenn Jonas
Associate Dean, College of Arts and Sciences
Charles Howard Professor of Religion
Campbell University

"Sherrill Stevens' work on the Gospel of John is both a worthy effort and a wonderful tool in the interpretation of the Fourth Gospel. I found *A Study Companion on the Gospel of John: Exposition, Interpretation, and Commentary* to be exactly what the title promises. While Stevens provides an excellent recounting of the events and teachings of the gospel in his exposition material, it was in the interpretation and commentary sections that I found the greatest blessing. He challenges the easy, traditional reading and re-reading of John with several novel suggestions. Whether or not one agrees with his conclusions, even nontraditional conclusions are presented in a gracious way that invites intellectual and spiritual conversation with the text. This book is a blessing in the ways it invites an expanded reflection on the Gospel of John."

Alan Ray
Senior Pastor, Ridge Baptist Church
Richmond, Virginia

"In this commentary, Dr. Stevens provides the reader with sound biblical exegesis and exposition, thoughtful devotional insights, and practical implications on the Gospel of John. I recommend this volume written by one who not only studies the New Testament, but also lives by its words and wisdom."

Marion D. Lark
Retired Minister
Henderson, North Carolina

Contents

Page 5
A Momentous Beginning
(John 1:1-51)

Page 13
The Early Ministry by Jesus
(John 2:1–4:54)

Page 27
The "I Am" Revelations
(John 5:1–11:57)

Page 59
Nearing the End
(John 12:1-50)

Page 69
The Last Evening
(John 13:1–17:26)

Page 93
Arrogant Power in Action
(John 18:1–19:42)

Page 105
Assurance, Hope, Guidance
(John 20:1–21:25)

Dedication

To Marguerite,
Faithful Christian
Lifelong Soulmate

Introduction

There are no documents that have been more influential in the culture of Western civilization than the four Gospels of the Christian New Testament. Each gospel has features that make it unique and distinctive.

- Matthew and Luke have the lovely but different nativity stories.
- Matthew has the incomparable collection of teachings called the Sermon on the Mount, a collection of parables of the Kingdom, and the global Great Commission in the concluding verses of the final chapter.
- Mark has the unique position of being the first written, and of being most simply a narrative account of where Jesus goes and what he does.
- Luke is the most universal, focusing on the compassion of Jesus for the underprivileged and outcasts of society, and the inclusion of all people along with the Israelites—in the embrace of God's outreach to mankind.
- John has major differences from the Synoptics, in what it includes and does not include, and in the way it treats both events and teachings.

The Fourth Gospel is anonymous in the text. According to tradition, the writer is the apostle John, son of Zebedee and brother of James, and his identity is suggested by the reference to "the disciple whom Jesus loved." That authorship has been widely questioned among contemporary interpreters, however. The dating for the writing varies by different researchers from CE 90 to CE 150. Even at CE 90 the apostle would have been of advanced age well beyond the normal life expectancy in that time. The question of time and authorship is made more involved by the tradition that the author of the gospel is also the author of the three Johannine epistles and the apocalypse in the Book of Revelation.

The traditions about authorship and place of writing include that the apostle John in his last years lived and preached in Ephesus and that he was the John exiled on the isle of Patmos, probably during the Domitian persecution of Christians in that area during the decade of the 90s CE (Rev. 1:9). It is widely believed that there was also a John the Elder who lived and actively served in the area of Ephesus during that same period. Some interpreters have used the identification of the writer of the second and third Johannine epistles as "the elder" to indicate that John the Elder wrote all five of the Johannine documents.

Two characteristics of the Fourth Gospel seem to favor the apostle as its writer. One, there are many references to first-person kinds of information and details about daily incidents in the life of Jesus. Two, much of the emphasis, in descriptions of what Jesus does and in interpretation of what he teaches, focuses on the meaning of his actions and teachings. That emphasis on details indicates first-person familiarity. Personal involvement is also indicated by the writer's use of the concept of "signs" to indicate that the act or the teaching is a clear reflection of Jesus' identity and the nature of his mission in incarnation.

References found among writings by early church fathers describe this gospel as being a product of the two Johns, both apostle and elder, or some associates of the apostle, or possibly even someone with help from the congregation of the Ephesian church. Taking all these involved factors into account, William Barclay sets forth a convincing possibility in the introduction to his popular and helpful commentary on this John.[1]

Barclay suggests that the aged apostle provided the information and insights recorded in the gospel, and that John the Elder, or their younger associates or assistants, actually wrote the document. Among other things, this helps solve the problem of the apostle's possibly boastful reference to himself as the "disciple whom Jesus loved" (i.e., "I" was his favorite); that is, if the reference is made by others in admiration of the devotion and faithfulness of the aged saint.

So, we have before us this magnificent document. It is the most loved, most quoted, and most often read by many Christians. The writer clearly declares his purpose in writing: "these are written that you may believe that Jesus is the Christ, the Son of God, and that believing you may have life in his name" (20:31). This gospel is an avowedly theological writing. In it we find many great concepts about the nature and character of God, the reason for God's self-revelation in incarnation, the dynamic meaning of God's ever-present inspiration and guidance in human life, and the undergirding grace that gives assured hope about eternal life. These concepts are so infinitely awesome that they are often beyond the capacity of finite minds to grasp, but they richly inform and deeply bless Christians who are enabled by enlightenment and grace to simply trust God.

NOTE

[1] William Barclay, *The Gospel of John, vol. 1* (Philadelphia: Westminster Press, 1956), xxxix-xli.

EDITOR'S NOTE

The biblical text is not printed. This is done with intent that this volume will be a companion for Bible study. The author believes that reading the text from a personal Bible, followed by considering the interpretation and commentary herein, will make this volume most helpful.

In the chapters that follow, the author's writing is divided into three sections:

1. Exposition (study or discussion of the biblical text; appears in regular text font)
2. **Interpretation (analysis or background on the biblical text; appears in bold type)**
3. *Commentary (editorial or application of the biblical text; appears in italics)*

OUTLINE OF THE GOSPEL OF JOHN

Chapter 1: From Creation to Incarnation
Chapter 2: Jesus Becomes Publicly Active
Chapter 3: New Life and God's Love
Chapter 4: The Nature of God and Worship
Chapter 5: A Healing and Discourse on Identity
Chapter 6: Loaves, Fishes, and the Bread of Life
Chapter 7: Controversy: Who Is This Jesus?
Chapter 8: Light, and Who Sees It
Chapter 9: Who Are the Really Blind?
Chapter 10: Shepherds, Gates, and Folds
Chapter 11: Truth and Power Collide
Chapter 12: Coming to Jerusalem
Chapter 13: "As I Have Done to You"
Chapter 14: Promise of Ongoing Presence
Chapter 15: Fruitful Life, Witnessed by Love
Chapter 16: Counsel Before Departure
Chapter 17: Divine Intercession
Chapter 18: Evil Designs in Progress
Chapter 19: Corrupt Power Seems to Win
Chapter 20: God, Good, and Life Are Triumphant
Chapter 21: Love Me, Feed My Lambs

A Momentous Beginning

(John 1:1-51)

THE WORD WAS GOD
(1:1)

The Gospel of John begins with a majestic prologue. Its sweep covers the period from before the existence of the material universe until the time of the incarnate ministry of Jesus of Nazareth. John introduces the concept of *LOGOS* (Word), which is not present in the other gospels. This gospel does not include a nativity story.

The LOGOS term is in current use among Greek philosophers. Aristotle uses the term to mean "reasoned discourse." Stoic philosophers identify it with the "animating principle" of the universe. John uses the term to refer to the Son of God who becomes incarnate as Jesus of Nazareth.

…

Use of the English term WORD to translate the Greek term LOGOS conveys its own meaning for our trying to understand the first verses of the prologue to John. "Word" is a primary vehicle of communication between persons. A person's "word" begins as an idea, desire, or intent within the inner self before it becomes a spoken expression to another and the basis for understanding, relationship, and/or action.

The relation of Word to God is inseparable. The proclamation being made by John is that the Word which becomes flesh in the person of Jesus is one and inseparable from the thinking, designing, planning, and acting of God in the creation of all that exists. Jesus is always clear that what Father, Son, and Spirit think, intend, design, and do are one and the same.

…

THE UNITY OF GOD
(1:2-5)

John begins with a majestic proclamation about infinite beginnings. The focus of verses 1-14 is to set the stage for the proclamation of the Incarnation. Verses 1-3 describe the Word as present within the unity of God from the beginning and in God's creative action. Verses 4-5 describe "him" (the Word) as having the essence of life and being the source of life and light for mankind.

John's identification of Jesus as the Word, sharing in the fullness of God, sets the stage for his later use of "signs" to indicate that the words and deeds of Jesus reveal that he is indeed the divine Son of God. Central to the nature of the Eternal Son is the very essence of life ("in him was life," v. 4). As a reference to the dynamic effect of the Incarnation, this life in the Son will be light for humankind that will shine in the darkness, and darkness will not overcome it (v. 5). The word here is a form of the verb *katalamban*.[1] Abbott-Smith translates *katalambano* as "lay hold of, comprehend."[2] Bauer cites this use of katelaben as "did not grasp."[3] These meanings focus on the inability of "darkness" to understand and make us of "light." The focus of the passage is on the contrast of light and darkness, the triumph of light over darkness, and the inability of darkness to eliminate (put out) the light.[4]

Most traditional interpretations of verse 5 present light and darkness as entities that are antagonistic to and in competition with each other. A more correct understanding is that light and darkness are conditions that are by nature opposites (prevailing truth and grace *versus* dominating arrogance and self-centeredness). Where one is, the other cannot be. English translations reflect two different understandings of the meaning of this verse:

1. The darkness of sinful humanity ("He came unto his own and his own received him not," 1:11) is not powerful enough to overcome and eliminate the light ("But to all who received him . . . he gave power to become sons of God," 1:12).
2. The darkness that sinfulness creates in human life so blinds untransformed persons to the light that they are unable to comprehend, grasp, take hold of that light ("The true light . . . was in the world . . . but the world knew him not," 1:9-10).

Note these examples that confirm both of the above meanings are equally true:

- "comprehended it not" (KJV)
- "has not understood it" (NIV)
- "has not overcome it" (KJVII RSV NRSV)
- "not overpowered it" (NIV footnote)
- "has not put it out" (The Message and The Good News Bible)
- "has not extinguished it" (The Living Bible)
- "has never quenched it" (The New English Bible)

. . .

The light of true life that Jesus reveals when "The Word becomes flesh and dwells among us" (1:14) has never been put out by all the darkness created by people who choose self-centeredness instead of trust in God, choosing "I'll go my own way" instead of following Jesus in the way of life to abundant life. The light of grace and life shines brightly in the face of Jesus Christ. It is also glaringly true that those who "love(d) darkness . . . because their deeds are evil" (3:19) are not able to comprehend, grasp, understand, lay hold on the light that Jesus gives. It is with divine insight that Jesus tells Nicodemus, "Unless one is born anew (from above), he cannot see the kingdom of God" (3:3). The word translated as "see" is idein, the infinitive of orao, meaning "to see, perceive, grasp the meaning of." Apart from a transforming conversion wrought by the grace of God, a sinful person cannot even "get the idea of" what it means to live "in the light" that comes into the world when "the Word becomes flesh"; when Jesus, "though he was in the form of God, did not count equality with God a thing to be grasped (clung to and held onto), but emptied himself, taking the form of a servant, being born in the likeness of men" (Phil. 2:6-7). For those who choose darkness, the light is incomprehensible. The contextual emphasis that darkness has not been able to "put out" the light seems most appropriate in the Prologue.

...

A PREPARING WITNESS
(1:6-8)

John the Baptist is introduced as a man sent from God whose role is to bear witness to the great source of light and life being proclaimed. This forerunner witness is forthright in his declaration that he is not the light but that his role is to identify the one who is the Light so that people can know him and believe in him.

This role for John the Baptist as a forerunner witness about the coming light has an anticipating heritage. After the Babylonian Exile ends the kingdom era of Israelite history, a messianic hope develops. Post-exilic Jews dream of a new son of David, a divinely anointed king who will restore their nation to unity, prominence, and prosperity (Ezek. 37:21-28). They believe that Elijah, who was taken into heaven without dying (2 Kgs. 2:11), will be sent to prepare for the cataclysmic beginning of the messianic age (Mal. 4:5). John the Baptist is believed to be the fulfillment of that hope; he will identify Jesus as the Messiah.

AN EVENT WITH ETERNAL PURPOSE
(1:9-13)

The writer continues his proclamation with a paragraph about what is happening, but he writes from the perspective of one who knows the end of the story. The Word, the divine source of light and life, comes into the world of humankind. The writer describes how the very Maker of the world is not recognized in this place where he surely belongs, by people who had received life and light from him. The light has its impact, nevertheless. Those who do see, who believe and receive, have a transformation of life and enter a new relationship with God.

> The KJV and NIV translations of verse 11 differ from the RSV and some other translations and paraphrases. The Greek text has forms of the basic word *idios*, which is a simple possessive. The first "his own" is *idia* (neuter plural), which refers to a general possessive relationship with things, while the second "his own" is *idioi* (masculine plural), which refers to a relationship with people.[5] Translations such as "his own realm," "his own things," and "his own home" in the first statement, and "his own people" in the second are appropriate interpretations. The initiative of the Word in coming to enlighten mankind does not end in futility, however, for some do receive him, believe in him, and become children of God through faith and a new birth of spirit.

A NEW REVELATION
(1:14-18)

The momentous truth of incarnation is written in simple but awesome words. The Word who is infinite, divine, creative source of all that exists, source of life and light, becomes a human person and lives a physical life among humankind. People see him live and hear him teach. The writer describes him as "the only Son from the Father." John the Baptist bears witness of him as "the coming one." He brings a new revelation of grace and truth, in contrast to the religion of law and ritual that came through Moses. The Son makes the Father known in a new and personal way.

> This is an appropriate place to consider what it means that Jesus is the "only/only begotten" Son. The Greek word is *monogenes*, a compound word formed from *monos* (only) and *gennao* (to sire a child). The basic meaning is to beget a single child. It correctly describes Jesus as "only Son." Questions arise, however, by the addition of "begotten" to the description. The church fathers debate it for four centuries. There are also plural descriptions of "sons/children of God" in the New Testament (See John 1:12, 1 John 3:1-2, and others.) The compound word was also used to mean "unique/only one of a kind."[6] The translations "unique Son," or "only divine Son" to describe Jesus, and "sons/children of God by faith" (Gal. 3:26) to describe Christians, are preferred as more accurate.
>
> John writes looking back at what they have experienced in the life of Jesus. Jesus lives truth and grace by example. He reveals a quality of glory, a divine quality that belongs to him as the Eternal Son. "We all" (a witness for the Christian community) receive grace from the one who is full of grace, and though no human persons have seen God, the Son makes God known to them.

...

A vital and transforming truth is declared in the statement that "The law was given through Moses; grace and truth came through Jesus Christ." There is a distinctive difference in the way people thought about the character of God before Jesus lives and after he "makes the Father known." The Law, which came through Moses, is centered in God as a Sovereign who requires obedience for approval, and who is believed to require chastisement to satisfy justice for any failure to meet every ritual of the law. Jesus reveals for us that God is Heavenly Father. God's heart is outgoing in a quest to forgive and reconcile. God's very nature is caring love. The character of God and the purpose of religion, as Jesus reveals them, are distinctively different from the pre-incarnation tenets of Old Testament Judaism. The Fourth Gospel is a wonderfully inspiring record of how the wonders of this beginning prologue are lived out and taught by Jesus of Nazareth, the Word who became flesh and dwelt among us (see 2 Cor. 4:6).

...

JOHN'S TRANSITIONAL ROLE
(1:19-23)

John the Baptist's preaching in the wilderness is an occasion for the Jewish religious leaders to send inquirers to check him out. John identifies himself as one whose role is to prepare for the coming messiah. He cites an Isaiah passage (40:3-5) as the prophetic basis for his preaching.

> By the time Jesus lives there has developed among the Jews a very active anticipation that the long-hoped-for Messiah will surely come at any time. Because many Jews expect the Messiah to be a victorious military leader who will free them from the occupying Romans, every revolutionary insurrectionist is thought to be "the Coming One" (see Acts 5:34-37). Every popular religious proclaimer is thought to be Elijah, who is expected as a forerunner to come again just before the Messiah, as the "preparer of the way" (Matt. 16:14).

JOHN'S BAPTISM
(1:24-28)

The inquirers next question John about his authority for baptizing. John declares that his baptism is a part of preparing for the Coming One who is already present but unrecognized, one who is unbelievably superior to him.

> John's preaching and baptizing confuse the religious leaders in Jerusalem. In Old Testament Judaism the Jews practice immersion as a ritual to cleanse "Gentile uncleanness" from any Gentile who wishes to become a Jewish proselyte. The priests are the proper ones to do ritual baptizing, and John the Baptist is not a priest. The people John is baptizing are Jews, not Gentiles. Why, then, does John baptize?

JOHN IDENTIFIES JESUS
(1:29-34)

John's first identification of Jesus personally is as "the Lamb of God." He says that Jesus was identified to him as God's anointed by the dove at his baptism. He is instructed that this one will baptize with the Holy Spirit.

> John's gospel does not record the baptism of Jesus, nor does it have an explanation of the reason for Jesus being baptized. He has no need of ritual cleansing, nor does Jesus need to repent and bring forth fruits of repentance as a witness of changed life before baptism. John the Baptist speaks of that baptism as an event already done. In his description of Jesus' baptism, John describes the awesome glory of it and the witness it gives of the one who is present among them. This record of witness by John does not identify the hearers. John describes Jesus as the Lamb of God who takes away the sin of the world, but he does not explain how that saving grace is accomplished.

...

The description of Jesus as the Lamb of God is one of several related theological beliefs scattered throughout the Bible. Traditional Christianity came to understand that Jesus, by his death on the cross, fulfilled the Jewish belief that the ritual sacrifice of a lamb (slaughter and sprinkling blood on an altar) accomplished an "atonement" (covering over and satisfying the divine requirement for justice and appropriate punishment for human sinfulness before forgiveness could be given). That understanding and belief are problematic for me for two reasons.

I find no indication that Jesus ever hinted that dying as an atoning sacrifice was the purpose for or the resulting outcome of the incarnation. Other references to Jesus as the "sacrificial Lamb" are found in 1 Peter 1:19, Hebrews 9:12, and predominantly in the Book of Revelation (which is highly figurative in nature). Other references to cleansing the guilt offering for sin, being an expiation for sin, etc. were interpretations by the varied writers. I am most convinced by the absence of "atoning sacrifice" in the language of Jesus.

The writer does not include a record about John's preaching that describes the meaning of his baptism. All three Synoptic Gospels record that John required "works of repentance as evidence of moral life" before baptism (Matt. 3:8, Mark 1:4, Luke 3:8). That is a different meaning for baptism in contrast to Jewish immersion of proselytes to cleanse the ritual impurity of being Gentile. This is evidence that John the Baptist was a transitional figure in the marked change from Judaism to the new revelation of Jesus.

...

John again affirms the superior status of Jesus and again tells of his role as a preparing forerunner. In his witness about the baptism of Jesus, John declares that he has done it by divine assignment. He also witnesses that the identity of Jesus is confirmed by the Spirit's descent upon him. Note how the writer records events about Jesus and shows how they are "signs" that gave clear evidence of who Jesus is as the incarnate Son of God.

THE FIRST FOLLOWERS OF JESUS
(1:35-51)

John the Baptist already has a group of disciples following him. He identifies Jesus to two of them as the Lamb of God. They go to get acquainted with Jesus and become his followers. One is Andrew, who then brings his brother Simon to Jesus. Andrew refers to Jesus as Messiah. He apparently has gotten that understanding from John, though it is not so stated in the text. Jesus calls Simon Cephas (Peter), Cephas means "rock" in Aramaic, and Petros means "rock" in Greek.

Jesus plans to go to Galilee. Before leaving he seeks out Philip who is from the Galilean city of Bethsaida, as are Andrew and Simon Peter. Their close association indicates that Philip is also among the disciples of John the Baptist. Jesus invites Philip to come with them, so Philip goes to invite Nathanael to come also. When Philip tells Nathanael that they believe Jesus of Nazareth is the hoped-for Messiah, Nathanael replies with a harsh question: "Can anything good come out of Nazareth?" There is no explanation for his scornful attitude about Nazareth, though he is from Cana near Nazareth (see John 21:2). Perhaps there have been earlier bad experiences. Philip simply asks Nathanael to come and see for himself.

Nathanael approaches Jesus and is surprised when Jesus commends him as a man without guile. Whether the others have told Jesus about him, or if Jesus reflects extraordinary insight, the comment amazes Nathanael. He responds as though he believes Jesus is more than an ordinary man and addresses him as Son of God.

This event in Judea identifies five of the first disciples of Jesus. The unnamed disciple of John the Baptist (vv. 37, 40) may well be John, son of Zebedee and brother of James. The familiar stories from the Synoptic Gospels record the calling of Andrew, Simon Peter, James, and John as the first disciples, on the shores of the Sea of Galilee instead of in Jerusalem. In the Synoptics there is no record of a special calling of Philip and Nathanael, but they are included in the naming of the Twelve. James and John are not named at all in the Gospel of John, and they are identified only once as the sons of Zebedee (21:2). This tends to support the belief that the source of the information in the gospel is John, who chooses only to refer to "the disciple whom Jesus loved."

NOTES

[1] D. Eberhard Nestle, *Novum Testamentum Graece* (New York, American Bible Society, 1950), 230. See also Brooke Westcott and Fenton Hort, *The New Testament* (New York: MacMillan, 1946), 187.

[2] G. Abbot-Smith, *A Manual Greek Lexicon of the New Testament* (Edinburgh: T&T Clark, 1950), 235

[3] William F. Arndt and F. Wilbur Gingrich, eds., *Walter Bauer's, A Greek-English Lexicon of the New Testament* (Chicago: University of Chicago Press, 1979), 413.

[4] Wilbert Howard, "The Gospel of St. John, Exegesis," *The Interpreter's Bible, vol. 8,* (New York: Abingdon Press, 1952), 466-467.

[5] Edwyn C. Hoskyns, edited by Francis N. Davey, *The Fourth Gospel,* (London: Faber and Faber Limited, 1947), 146

[6] Arndt and Gingrich, *Bauer's Lexicon,* 527.

The Early Ministry by Jesus
(John 2:1–4:54)

THE WEDDING AT CANA (2:7-11)

Jesus and his disciples travel to Cana in Galilee where they attend a wedding. The writer does not identify the wedding party nor any relationship between them and Mary's family. The focus is on Jesus and his action. When the wine begins to give out, Mary tells Jesus—apparently expecting him to do something about it. Jesus replies, "What have you to do with me?" His statement that "his hour" has not yet come seems to indicate that he is not yet ready to begin doing supernatural acts that will stir messianic hope and lead to demonstrations. Nevertheless, he instructs servants to fill the purification jars, and take water from the jars to the steward of the feast. The water-turned-into-wine impresses the steward. This event is described as the first of the signs done by Jesus.

The statement by Jesus to his mother appears to be discourteous in English translation. William Barclay writes that the question is a common conversational expression that means "Leave it to me; I will take care of it."[1] The traditional understanding of Jesus' instruction is for the servants to take water from the jars they have just filled. John emphasizes the amount of water/wine by the number and size of the water pots. The same root word (*antleo*) for "draw/draw out" is used here and in John 4:7-11. From the root verb is also formed the noun for a bucket to draw from a well.[2] The verb itself suggests drawing from a well.[3]

On this basis some interpreters suggest that Jesus turns the whole well of water into wine. The only difference in meaning, however, is the difference in quantity, for anyone who can change water into wine can change a "well full" as well as several gallons. The idea of changing the well of water into wine has not been widely accepted, and a "well full" would not have been needed for the wedding. Enlargement of quantity may enhance the writer's purpose to indicate that the action by Jesus is indeed a sign that "manifests his glory" and leads to his disciples believing in him. I see no convincing difference.

A brief aside seems fitting here. The use of the concept "sign" is important for understanding the Fourth Gospel. Forms of the word *sameion* (a sign) occur with special meaning in this gospel. Seven times it refers to a specific "miraculous" action by Jesus (2:11 and 18, 4:54, 6:14, 9:16, 11:47, 12:18). Another ten times it refers to "miraculous acts" and "wonder works" in general.

Jay Green translates the word "signs," but he interprets the action as "miracles."[4] The KJV translates "miracles." The NIV translates "miraculous signs." The RSV translates "signs."

A "sign" is generally interpreted to mean "an item, event, or metaphor" that "points to or indicates" something beyond itself. Marcus Borg describes this with a play on words: "Signs . . . sign-ify something, and what they signify is their significance."[5] The writer of John uses the word "sign" to refer to actions by Jesus that "indicate, reveal" who Jesus is—the Eternal Son Incarnate. The signs are significant because they "manifest his glory" and lead his disciples to believe in him (2:11). On the other hand, they also lead his adversaries to fear him and determine to kill him (11:47-50).

A VISIT TO CAPERNAUM
(2:12)

Verse 12 records a visit by Jesus, his family, and his disciples to Capernaum for several days.

> The Synoptic Gospels record an event when Jesus is rejected and threatened in Nazareth as an apparent reason for going to Capernaum and making it a center of his movements in the Galilee region (Matt. 13:54-58, Mark 6:1-6, Luke 4:16-30). The Gospel of John does not include this event and, as we have noted, records more of ministry activity in Judea.

PASSOVER IN JERUSALEM
(2:13-25)

John 2 records one of two Passover visits Jesus makes to Jerusalem (John 2:13, 11:55). He cleanses the Temple, accusing the keepers of the Temple of turning that holy place into a house of trade. The Jews (Jewish leaders) challenge his authority for his action. Jesus compares the coming destruction of the Temple to his own coming death and declares that he will arise after three days. The writer summarizes that many believe in Jesus, but he does not "trust himself to them" because he "knew what was in man(kind)."

> The Synoptics record only one Passover visit by Jesus to Jerusalem: the week when Jesus is crucified (Matt. 26:17-19, Mark 14:12-16, Luke 22:7-13). This incident is also unique to John for it records a cleansing of the Temple early in his public ministry. The Synoptics, by contrast, record the Temple cleansing near the end of his life, on the Sunday of the entry into Jerusalem (Matt. 21:12, Luke 19:45), or the next day (Mark 11:12). It has been suggested that Jesus did a second cleansing at the end of his ministry, but there is no recorded evidence to support it. It seems most likely that the record in John is placed here to support the writer's emphasis on signs, or placed here in later copying for that purpose.

The records, however, are similar. Jesus finds merchandising going on in the Temple area. The original purpose of buying and selling near the Temple had been beneficial, making available to pilgrims approved animals for the sacrifices to be offered and the specified Jewish coins required for the Temple tax. Competition apparently has caused the operations to move closer and closer to the Temple until they have moved into the very Temple itself (or sacred Temple courts). Jesus demonstrates a deep devotion to the holy purpose of the Temple and a righteous indignation at its corruption for material gain.

The Jewish authorities challenge Jesus for his cleansing of the Temple. After all, according to their Jewish tradition, the control and maintenance of the Tabernacle/Temple had been assigned to the tribe of Levi by Moses at Sinai. According to the authorities, since Jesus is of the tribe of Judah and not a Levite nor a priest, he has no authority to do what he has done. As is his pattern, Jesus does not debate matters of Mosaic regulation with his adversaries. Many times he simply responds with a question that they cannot answer and that totally confounds them.

In the Synoptics, Jesus describes the reason for his action as the gross violation they have made of the sacred purpose of the Temple. In this Fourth Gospel record, Jesus gives them an example they cannot understand by using the Temple as a metaphor for a reference to his coming death and resurrection. This interchange seems to indicate that the event belongs more properly, as with the Synoptic Gospels, at the later time during the Passion Week events.

The writer includes a summary statement to conclude the record of this trip to Jerusalem. This event is early in his public ministry. The response by Jesus reflects his pattern of not encouraging messianic demonstrations.

...

As you read the Gospels, note how Jesus damps down any tendency among the crowd toward messianic demonstrations. There are two reasons for this: Jesus knows that any such demonstrations will be severely quelled by the Romans. Jesus also tries to help the people learn that he has not come to be the military conqueror to drive out the Romans that the Jewish nation has long dreamed of and hoped for.

...

JESUS AND NICODEMUS
(3:1-12)

The familiar story about Nicodemus is not described as a part of the Passover festival event, but it apparently takes place in Jerusalem. The latter part of John 3 has Jesus still in the Judean area (v. 22).

Nicodemus comes to see Jesus out of genuine interest in his teachings and having been impressed by the "signs." Jesus turns the focus away from mere teachings to the more fundamental matter of faith and the effect of faith on a person's life. Jesus tells Nicodemus, "unless one is born anew (from above), he/she cannot see the kingdom of God" (v. 3), nor "enter the kingdom of God" (v. 5).

Nicodemus is confused by the reference to birth, thinking about physical birth. Jesus tells Nicodemus that unless a person is born of water (physical birth), and the Spirit (spiritual new birth) he/she cannot enter the kingdom of God. Nicodemus is amazed and puzzled, and asks, "How can this be?" In verses 10-12 Jesus talks to Nicodemus about the distinction between earthly things and heavenly things.

Nicodemus is a Pharisee and a Jewish official (ruler, member of the Sanhedrin, see John 7:32-53). He does not agree with fellow Pharisees who oppose Jesus so harshly. He later assists Joseph of Arimathea in the hasty burial of Jesus after the Crucifixion (John 19:39). Nicodemus' confusion about birth (physical/spiritual) is a common problem.

People have always had difficulty forming a concept of spirit without physical form. Jesus makes it clear that he is not referring to physical birth, but to a transforming spiritual experience that will cause a person to become a new person.

The word translated "see" (*idein*) is the root from which our English word "idea" is derived, and one of its primary usages is "to perceive" (as in, "Oh, now I see"). Jesus makes a distinction for Nicodemus by referring to both birth "of water" and "of Spirit." By physical birth we become a human person. By spiritual new birth we come into a new relationship with God.

...

The "kingdom of God" to which Jesus refers is not a geographical area ruled over by a king, nor a "realm in heaven" after physical death. Instead, it is a relationship with God. Persons who are alienated from God, being out of harmony with God through sinfulness, are consequently not "in the kingdom of God," not accepting the sovereignty of God in their lives. These differing concepts of kingdom, such as the distinction between physical birth and spiritual new birth, are a result of our human difficulty in forming and describing spiritual realities for which we have no adequate language. This difficulty underlies the ancient practice of pagan idolatry.

Divine spirits were believed to inhabit physical objects such as heavenly bodies, certain animals, carved idols, and even trees and stone pillars. The Bible includes many physical references to God, who is Infinite Supernatural Spirit. Because we have physical bodies and live in a material environment, we tend to think with that orientation: we simply do not have words in our language to describe spiritual realities. Thinking spiritually requires of us a conscious and intentional refocus. It is only by the Holy Spirit's helping that we are enabled to "see" spiritual things.

...

THE CENTRAL ROLE OF FAITH
(3:13-15)

Bible versions that form the text into paragraphs most often include verses 13-15 with the Nicodemus conversation. Traditional interpretations (as in red-letter editions) continue the speaking of Jesus through verse 21. Note that the subject changes at verse 13, and verses from 13 through 21 utilize the grammatical third person as commentary by the writer. This is, nevertheless, the most familiar passage in this entire gospel and it gives voice to as great truth as has ever captured the human mind. Faith, and its dynamic effect in human life, is the theme of these introductory verses.

The writer describes the Son of Man as the only one who has ascended to heaven, having also descended from heaven. The wilderness incident about "fiery serpents" and the "bronze serpent" (Num. 21:4-9) is used to describe the elevation (lifting up) of an object of faith as a source of healing in the wilderness, and as the way of receiving "eternal life" through "believing in Jesus."

In the incident about fiery serpents in the wilderness (Num. 21:4-9) the people complain about their circumstances and Moses' leadership. Moses declares that their grouching and complaining show lack of faith in God. The fiery serpents are described as God's chastisement for their distrust. The bronze serpent is set up as an object of faith by which the people can be brought back into trust in God and to healing from serpent bites. This is for the Israelites a lesson about the central importance of faith in their relationship with God. The stated comparison about "believing in the Son of Man" is an introductory reference to the following verses describing the vital and eternal importance of God's grace and human faith.

GOD'S LOVE AND OUR FAITH
(3:16-21)

The love of God (*agape*) led to the Incarnation (John 1:14, Phil. 2:5-8). The divine action in incarnation sets the focus. The purpose of the Incarnation is about "whoever believes." The result is about whether a person "perishes" or has "eternal life." The description that follows in John (vv. 17-21) is about God's purpose in the Incarnation, to condemn or to save. It is about people, to believe or not to believe, to love light or darkness, to love evil and hide in darkness or to come by faith into the light.

The use of *agape* to describe God's love focuses this passage on the outreaching, unselfish, benevolent character of God. It was his caring love that motivated the Incarnation. The human response described is about faith.

The outcome described is whether a person believes and has eternal life, or does not believe and perishes.

The use of the word perish is revealing. In Greek it translates apoletai (*apollumi*, root meaning "to be destroyed, to lose one's life").[6] In the Septuagint (LXX), a Greek translation of Hebrew, it replaces aBaDh (root meaning "to wander and lose oneself").[7] The concept is about losing by deprivation, not as a punishment.

...

The description of Jesus as the one who "has ascended into heaven" after having "descended from heaven" puts the focus of the writer into the time after the Ascension. (Some documents add at the end of verse 13 "who is in heaven." Many researchers believe this is an early explanatory addition.) The bronze serpent of Numbers 21:8-9 and the exalted (lifted up) Son of Man are both set forth as objects of faith, for it was/is "whoever believes" that causes an effect in a person's life. Understanding the statement about "being lifted up" as a reference to crucifixion is not supported by the focal context of this passage.

The awesome proclamation of verse 16 declares the universal embrace of God's intent to reconcile to harmony all alienated persons who will respond in trusting faith to the revelation God is making in Christ. Do not overlook the emphasis Jesus makes about the unanimity there is between himself and the Father in the purpose of the Incarnation and the work he is doing in the Incarnation. The purpose of incarnation is not condemnation of sinfulness (v. 17). Human sinfulness is the alienating thing that separates from God and causes a person to perish apart from God. God makes a choice to become incarnate in Jesus, to reveal that God is a God of love, so alienated sinners can become reconciled to harmony with God through trusting faith.

Note that the focus in all of John 3 is about a life-transforming experience by which a "lost" person becomes a "saved" person. From the "you must be born again" (v. 7) words to Nicodemus to the declaration about "one who loves the light walking in the light" (v. 21), John 3 is about what happens within a person and what it means in a person's relationship with God.

According to the Gospels, Jesus teaches that human persons have an active role to play in the transforming experience called salvation. Both Matthew 4:17 and Mark 1:14-15 record that the central focus of preaching by Jesus is "repent and believe the gospel," both being dynamic, life-changing experiences that rise out of the deepest soul of a person resulting from trusting faith in the God revealed in Jesus. Jesus also teaches that it is the Holy Spirit, God present with us, leading to conviction and conversion, that makes divine grace become a saving reality in a person's life.

This experience is far different from a passive "Let go and let God have his way." It is an awesome truism that we cannot do it without God (his grace and forgiveness), and God will not do it without us (our active commitment in repentant faith). Not even Jesus will do it for you, but he will surely do it with you if you will choose to "repent and believe the gospel."

...

JESUS AND JOHN AND BAPTISM
(3:22-30)

Jesus and his disciples leave Jerusalem and go east down the Jericho Road through the Judean countryside to the Jordan valley between Jericho and the Dead Sea. There is no certain identification of Aenon and Salim, but in John 1:28 the lower Jordan area is recorded as the site of John's baptizing. The presence of Jesus and John the Baptist in the same area develops into a source of conversation among the people.

There is recorded no explanation about the "purifying" question (v. 25). The discussion, however, leads to questions about the relation of John and Jesus who are both baptizing (though in John 4:1 it is recorded that Jesus did not do the baptizing himself). John replies in a humble, self-effacing way and focuses on the importance of Jesus, using the relationship of himself as a friend of the bridegroom Jesus. John makes the familiar summary statement, "He must increase, but I must decrease."

The reference to purifying and baptism is a discussion with John about the Jewish practice of immersing Gentiles, who wished to become Jewish proselytes, to cleanse them ritually of their Gentile uncleanness.

A SUMMARY
(3:31-36)

Either John or the writer includes a commentary paragraph. He describes the one from above, Jesus, who is above all, who speaks for God, gives the Spirit, and represents the Father. He describes the one who "belongs to the earth," John, who speaks of human things. A summary sentence declares that human destiny depends on whether a person believes in and obeys this "Son" who has come from above.

...

Hebrews 1:1 has an inspired summary, "In many and varied ways God spoke of old to our fathers . . . but in these last days he has spoken to us by a Son." From God's ancient call to Abraham, in his leadership through Moses, and the proclamations of the prophets the vital role of faith is central to the development of Hebrew religion.

In the Incarnation, God makes a self-revelation of his infinite, outreaching love for all humanity, and his compassionate, forgiving aspiration to draw us all to himself in reconciling grace. God's saving grace can become real, however, only in persons whose very nature and life become transformed by trusting faith and divine grace. The central message of Jesus is, "repent and believe the gospel." Repentant faith is the central, reconciling, saving response for sinful human persons.

Some explanation needs to be written about "the wrath of God." The reference in verse 36 is the only recorded use of "the wrath of God" in the Gospels, and the context indicates that it is not spoken here by Jesus. The recorded use by Jesus of the word "wrath" is in an apocalyptic passage (Luke 21:23) where the subject is the horrible suffering in the destruction of Jerusalem, which was an expected tragedy that would happen before the establishment of the victorious messianic kingdom. The city is actually destroyed by the Romans in AD 70, earlier than the writing of John's gospel.

The Greek word that appears in both John 3:36 and Luke 21:23 is orge. The most prominent use of the words ZaYiM *(Hebrew)* and orge *(Greek)* throughout the Bible refers to wrath (anger) as the divine reaction against the sinful rebellion and disobedience of humankind. There is also a contrasting thread of meaning that runs through the Bible. G. Abbott-Smith records a primary root meaning of orge as "propensity of disposition."[8] When the Israelites forsake God to put their faith in and offer sacrifices to pagan idols, God does not excuse their unfaithfulness and protect them from the consequences of their choices and actions. Isaiah wrote (61:8), "I the Lord love justice . . . I will faithfully give them their recompense." The "propensity of disposition" revealed by God, however, is loving kindness and reconciling compassion.

When the Israelite kingdoms are destroyed and the people are scattered and exiled, Ezekiel writes that God will not forsake them and will gather them again, cleanse them from their uncleanness, and put a new heart and spirit in them (36:24-29).

Hosea 11 describes the heart-cry of God's love for his people and his compassionate intent to reconcile and restore them. In the allegory of Hosea's recovery of his unfaithful wife Gomer he writes, "I will allure her . . . bring her into the wilderness . . . speak tenderly to her . . . betroth you to me forever . . . in righteousness and in justice, in steadfast love, and in mercy (2:14, 19-20).

There is no more wonderfully graphic affirmation about God's character of caring love than the assurance offered in Psalm 23:6, "Surely, goodness and mercy shall follow me all the days of my life, and I shall dwell in the house of the Lord forever." The dynamic of that assurance is reflected in the primary meaning of the root word RaDaPh *"to follow earnestly, to pursue."*[9]

The "propensity of disposition" revealed by God is not wrath, but yearning to recover, restore, and reconcile. Our sinfulness breaks God's heart, but it does not make him want to destroy us. Paul writes that the purpose of God "in Christ . . . (was) . . . reconciling the world unto himself, not counting their trespasses against them (2 Cor. 5:19). That's not wrath; that's love and forgiveness.

. . .

MINISTRY IN GALILEE
(4:1-4)

Jesus leaves the Judean area to go to Galilee. John writes that at least part of the reason is to avoid being in competition with John the Baptist. Questions are developing about which of the two—Jesus or John—is gathering the largest following of disciples. In Samaria they arrive at Jacob's well near Sychar and stop for a lunch break to rest (the sixth hour).

The statement that to go to Galilee "he had to pass through Samaria" is significant. The geography south to north is Judea, Samaria, Galilee, but there is an interesting history behind it all.

When the Assyrian empire conquered the Northern Kingdom in 722 BCE, the captors took the leaders away into slavery and brought in Assyrians to keep the remaining population under control (2 Kgs. 17:24). Those taken away never returned, and those left behind intermarried with Canaanites. The Hebrew tribes of the Northern Kingdom thus became the Ten Lost Tribes of Israel. The resulting mixed race of Hebrews/Canaanites became known as the Samaritans who disputed with the remnant groups returning after the Babylonian exile (Ezra 4:1-4, Neh. 4:1-23).

Because of this history, the Jews of Jesus' day consider the Samaritans not true Jews and ritually unclean. They continue the practice developed by Jews traveling between Judea and Galilee on religious pilgrimages and for other reasons to "go around," in order to avoid any contact with Samaritans. From Judea they cross the Jordan to the east and travel north through Perea and the Decapolis before crossing the Jordan again to the west into Galilee. They reverse the route to return north to south. Jesus does not follow this practice of avoidance.

In Samaria, Jesus and the disciples come to a place with ancient associations. Sychar is in the same area as Shechem, an area with much history from the times of Jacob and the descendants of Joseph. Jacob's well is to Jews a sacred place. The description of Jesus as being weary reflects his true humanity (incarnation means infinite deity and finite mortality in one awesome person).

...

Incarnation is a mystery indeed. In Jesus, God reveals himself as a living human person and shows the divine qualities of love and grace that are infinite in the character of God. Remember that we are created in the image of God. Just as infinite divine spirit and physical human body are one in Jesus, likewise finite human spirit and physical body are one in each of us. At physical death our mortal body dies and our spirit goes to be with God who gave it. We too are "fearfully and wonderfully made" (Ps. 139:14 KJV).

...

AT JACOB'S WELL
(4:5-26)

While Jesus rests at the well near Sychar, the disciples go into the city to buy food. A Samaritan woman comes to the well for water. Jesus asks her for a drink, which surprises her. Instead of discussing Jewish/Samaritan relations, Jesus turns the subject to living water. He explains the difference between physical water that lasts until thirst returns and living water that satisfies the spirit. The woman asks for that gift of water but does not grasp the meaning of the difference.

Jesus tells her to go bring her husband, but she says she has no husband. Her past is a subject of embarrassment, so she changes the subject with a question about religion: "Where is the correct place to worship?" Jesus explains that true worship is worship of the Father, and that true worship is in "spirit and truth," because God is spirit. The woman seems baffled and says that when the Messiah comes, he will reveal correct answers. Jesus responds that he is the expected one.

The presence of the woman at noontime is unusual. The usual practice is for women and girls to come for water near sundown in the cool of the evening. Some writers surmise that the Samaritan woman's multiple marriages, referred to later, make her somewhat outcast so she comes at a different time to avoid others. There is no hint of this in the text. It is also culturally unusual for Jesus and the woman to have a conversation. The woman is surprised, "For Jews have no dealings with Samaritans" (see explanation above about Jewish/Samaritan animosities). This entire incident shows how Jesus disregards some long-developed Jewish prejudices and ritual practices.

Jesus changes the focus of their conversation by turning from water in the well to "living" water, the gift of Spirit. The woman does not understand until Jesus describes the gift he offers as an inner "spring of water welling up to eternal life." She asks for that gift of living water, but still understands it to be water that satisfies physical thirst—"that I may not thirst, nor come here to draw."

The conversation changes again, this time to character and to worship. Jesus tells the woman to bring her husband, and this reveals facts about her past life. She has had five husbands and is now living with a man who is not her husband. She changes the subject—to religion.

"Sir, I perceive that you are a prophet. Where is the correct place for worship? On Mount Gerizim or in Jerusalem? The Samaritan place or the Jewish place?" (The Samaritans have built a temple on Mount Gerizim and established a place of worship there because they are not welcome in Jerusalem and its temple.)

In response to the woman's questions, Jesus declares a transforming truth. "Where" is not what matters in worship. Whether worship is authentic is what counts.

There is no more significant and truth-directing statement in the Bible than the declaration by Jesus that "God is spirit" and "those who worship him must worship in spirit and truth." The Samaritan woman in response affirms the messianic hope long held by both Jews and Samaritans. Jesus identifies himself to her as that messiah. John 4 is one of the most incredibly revealing records of revelation that Jesus makes about himself.

...

Many of the Jewish customs that have developed through their early history in both their culture and their religion devalue people (women, children, the poor, Gentiles, etc.). Their customs and rituals also sometimes misdirect the purpose of religion (Sabbath prohibitions, hand washings, etc.). Jesus corrects the focus of such customs to reveal a truer meaning for human conduct and relationships.

Jesus treats all people as God's people. He reveals that religion is about authentic worship and transformed lives. His declaration that God is spirit reveals that ultimate reality belongs to the realm of spirit, "for the things that are seen are transient (temporary, short-lived), but the things that are unseen are eternal" (2 Cor. 4:18). Everything we think about God, believe about God, and imagine about relationship with God in time and in eternity must be in harmony with that truth, if they are to be accurate.

God was spirit and was fully God before anything material existed. God is the Creator Source who accomplishes creation of all that exists out of nothing material that existed before. Human use of physical terms (eyes, hands, voice, heart) is our way to describe God because we have no other language to describe God, who is Eternal Supreme Spirit. God has always been "pure Spirit" except when he becomes incarnate in Jesus of Nazareth. He does that for our benefit, to reveal himself and his character more fully than humanity has been able to comprehend before. His purpose is to reconcile us to himself (2 Cor. 5:19).

...

JESUS AND THE SAMARITANS
(4:27-42)

The disciples return from their trip into town and are astonished to find Jesus in conversation with a woman—and a Samaritan woman at that. The woman leaves, goes into town, tells what has happened and asks the question, "Can this be the Messiah?" The curious crowd goes to check it out.

The conversation between Jesus and the disciples reflects the difference in human experience that results from physical concerns in contrast to spiritual experiences. The disciples' attention is on being tired and hungry from their travels. They urge Jesus to eat some lunch. Jesus replies that he has experienced satisfaction they do not yet know.

Jesus then teaches a marvelous and ever-present truth for the disciples and for us. Spiritual harvests are different from agricultural harvests, the latter of which are seasonal. Spiritual harvests are always in season.

The arrival of people from the town leads to an interchange between Jesus and the crowd. Different members of the group react differently. Some believe in Jesus simply because of the woman's witness. "He told me all that I ever did," is enough to persuade them that Jesus is indeed supernatural since he has that kind of knowledge about her. The interest of the crowd leads them to ask Jesus to stay with them awhile. During two days he remains and teaches. Many others believe in him, not because of the woman's story but because they have heard from Jesus himself. They declare that from his teaching they know he is the Savior.

This incident occurs early in the ministry of Jesus. The relatively new disciples are not yet able to experience the satisfaction of spiritual experiences. Jesus replies that fulfillment of his mission is like food to him. He describes spiritual harvests as being always a present reality. Sowing the seeds of the gospel should be going on always, and reapers should be harvesting wherever "ripe grain" is found. Sowers and reapers together should be always sharing the labor of sowing and the joy of harvest.

...

The statement in verse 26 by Jesus identifying himself as the Messiah is different from his hesitance at other times and places to let people spread that belief about him. This self-identification, plus the fact that this incident is recorded so early in his public ministry, has led some writers to question its accuracy—though it has not been widely questioned. The people say they are certain that Jesus is the Savior of the world. If this text is accurate, it shows that the people hear something from the teaching of Jesus that expands their belief about Messiah. They believe he is more than a Jewish deliverer; he is a universal Savior. This is important to the

Samaritans who live with the awareness that the Jews think of them as outside the covenants of Jewish hope. The larger vision and hope are surely present in the Gentile world by the time John's gospel is written.

...

ANOTHER SIGN, A HEALING
(4:43-54)

After the short period spent in or near Sychar, the disciples and Jesus continue their travel into Galilee. They apparently simply bypass Nazareth. John has no record of the rejection in Nazareth (see Luke 4:16-30). John does, however, record Jesus' statement about a prophet having no honor in his own country.

The disciples and Jesus go to Cana and on toward Capernaum. Word has gone before them that Jesus has come from Judea. The news includes accounts of the Judean ministry of Jesus. Pilgrims who have gone to Jerusalem for the Passover bring those reports back with them. In Capernaum, an official's son is healed. The writer calls this the second sign Jesus has done in Galilee.

This record about the healing of an official's son comes from a different tradition than the incident reported in Matthew 8 and Luke 7 about the healing of a centurion's paralyzed servant. All three gospels record the healing as occurring in Capernaum. This incident occurs in John's sequence of events earlier than the Synoptics. This is, in all three, the first record of a healing by Jesus of a person at a distance and not in his presence. All three accounts emphasize the vital role that faith plays in the healing event. They are very similar, but very different.

...

The writer of John concludes this account with a declaration of the role of "signs" in the ministry of Jesus. He records this as the "second sign" Jesus does in Galilee, the last sign he enumerates. For this writer, the supernatural things Jesus does show clearly "who he is" and "what he is about" in the world. Throughout this gospel the writer keeps showing how the awesome things he writes in the opening prologue are fulfilled in the living words and actions of Jesus, the Word who becomes flesh and dwells among us.

...

NOTES

[1] William Barclay, *The Gospel of John, vol. 1* (Philadelphia: Westminster Press, 1956), 82-83.

[2] G. Abbott-Smith, *A Manual Greek Lexicon of the New Testament* (Edinburgh: T&T Clark, 1950), 42. William F. Arndt and F. Wilbur Gingrich, eds., *Walter Bauer's, A Greek-English Lexicon of the New Testament,* (Chicago: University of Chicago Press, 1979), 76.

[3] Edwyn C. Hoskyns, ed. Francis N. Davey, *The Fourth Gospel* (London: Faber & Faber Ltd., 1947), 189.

[4] Jay P. Green, *The Interlinear Greek-English New Testament, vol. 4* (Peabody, MA: Hendrickson Publishers, 1985), 252, v. 11.

[5] Marcus J. Borg, *Reading the Bible Again for the First Time* (New York: Harper One, 2002), 204.

[6] Abbottt-Smith, *Lexicon,* 52. Bauer, *Lexicon,* 95a.

[7] Abbott-Smith, *Lexicon,* 52. Samuel P. Tregelles, *Gesenius' Hebrew and Chaldee Lexicon to the Old Testament Scriptures* (Grand Rapids: Eerdmans, 1950), 3a.

[8] Abbott-Smith, *Lexicon,* 322.

[9] Tregelles, *Gesenius' Hebrew and Chaldee Lexicon,* 758b.

The "I Am" Revelations
(John 5:1–11:57)

A HEALING
(5:1-9)

John 5 records a visit to Jerusalem by Jesus and the disciples. A healing takes place at the Bethzatha pool. The pool is noted for occasional "troubling of the water." A tradition has developed that whoever is first into the water after a "troubling of the water" will be healed of their infirmity. Crowds of invalids lie around the pool, hoping to be "first next time." Jesus approaches a man who has been waiting thirty-eight years. He asks if the man wants to be healed (made whole). The man replies that he has no helper and is unable to be first, so he really has no hope. Jesus tells him to rise and walk, and he does.

There are manuscript differences about this passage, but they do not affect the incident of healing or the teaching that followed it. The site references at the end of chapter 4 and at the beginning of chapter 6 indicate that chapter 5 is included here out of sequence. Chapter 4 ends with Jesus in Capernaum. Chapter 6 begins, "After this Jesus went to the other side of the Sea of Galilee." Chapter 5 is an entirely Jerusalem event without any record of travel to Judea and return. This sequential question takes nothing from the meaning of the various events. It simply reflects the difficulty in any attempt to sequence the flow of activity in the life of Jesus.

The record of this event does not state which of the Jewish feasts is being observed, and this is different from other feast references in John (2:23, 6:4, 7:2, 11:55, 13:1). Some interpreters who have made special study of the time sequences in this gospel conclude that the most likely feast in this passage is Pentecost. I know of no definitive evidence to answer this question.

The healing event happens near the sheep gate at a pool called Bethesda/Bethzatha, a large pool surrounded by covered porches. A periodic stirring in the water has long been believed to be caused by a local deity (in Jewish belief by an angel). Other sources attribute the stirring of the pool to intermittent flow from one of the springs that feed into the pool. Following different sources, some translations include verse 4 (KJV, NASB), while others omit it and refer to it in a note (NIV, CEV, RSV).

SABBATH CONTROVERSY
(5:9-18)

It is a Sabbath day. Some Jewish officials rebuke the healed man for carrying his pallet on the Sabbath. He replies that he is just doing what the man who has healed him told him to do. He does not know that the healer is Jesus, so he cannot identify him. In a later conversation, Jesus talks with the man and encourages him to not sin anymore. Once the man knows his healer is Jesus, he tells this to the Jewish officials. This incident becomes a part of the ongoing disapproval of Jesus by the Jewish religious authorities. Jesus does not reply to their accusations about what is proper to do on the Sabbath and what is unlawful. He tells them that what he is doing shows that he and the Father are present and actively working. The authorities now have more to accuse Jesus of—describing God as his Father—which makes them even more determined to get rid of him.

Proper Sabbath conduct is an ongoing reason for controversy between Jesus and the Jewish religious leaders. The Sabbath commandment in the Decalogue probably begins as a single imperative word declaring the Sabbath a sacred day. Two reasons are recorded for God's command to rest on the Sabbath.

Exodus 20:11 states that God commanded rest on the Sabbath because God rested on the seventh day at the end of the creation (Gen. 2:2). Deuteronomy 5:15 states that God commanded rest on the Sabbath to help Israelites remember they had been slaves in Egypt.

The multitude of commands and prohibitions being practiced by Pharisees in Jesus' lifetime reflects centuries of additions by priests and Levites who are called on by the people to answer questions about what is allowed and what is not allowed (the number 613 actions not allowed has been widely reported but also disputed). Jesus ignores some trivial restrictions, reinterprets the purpose of sabbath, and exposes Jewish rationalizing and inconsistency of practice. Sabbath controversy continues to be an unresolved dispute until the end of his life. As noted above, accusations of blasphemy also become a major issue for the Jewish leaders since they deny Jesus' sonship relation to the Father.

...

The sabbath controversy reveals a clear difference in understanding between Jesus and the Jewish leaders about the meaning of sabbath. For the Jews, sabbath has its foundation in Moses' teaching about God's command. Sabbath is to be kept holy because God commands it. To protect sabbath sanctity, the Jews believe sabbath observance must be defined by rules of ritual and behavior. They believe God is just and requires obedience or punishes with chastisement. Jesus teaches that God establishes the Sabbath for the benefit of people: "The sabbath was made for man, not man for the sabbath" (Mark 2:27). His consistent practice is to "do good" and "heal" on the Sabbath (Matt. 12:12, Luke 14:3). He says to the Pharisees that he (the Son of Man) "is lord even of the sabbath" (Mark 2:27). The difference between a rule to be obeyed and actions to enhance human life is a clear revelation Jesus makes by both his teaching and his practice.

...

JESUS AND THE FATHER
(5:19-47)

The remainder of John 5 is a lengthy discourse by Jesus on the overarching theme of relationship between the Son and the Father:

- Verses 19-20 speak of the active works of Father and Son.
- Verse 21 is a declaration that Father and Son are equally sources of human life.
- Verses 22-23 focus on the role of the Son in incarnation. Jesus says that the Father has given him the role of "judgment" so that he will be "honored" by people.
- In verse 24 Jesus affirms that whoever hears his teaching and trusts that it is authentic truth from God will have eternal life.
- In verses 25-29 Jesus speaks again about Father and Son as the source of life. In these verses he declares that this truth applies both before and after physical death.
- In the rest of the discourse, Jesus sets forth evidences of his unity with the Father and says his chosen actions and teaching are "just" because he is doing God's will. For anyone who does not trust his word (v. 31), there is the witness of John the Baptist who is widely accepted among them as "a shining light" (vv. 32-35).
- Jesus continues in verses 36-38 his claim to have even higher witness to his unity with the Father, declaring that his works and words are the same as the Father's. He charges that if the authorities cannot recognize his unity with the Father, they do not have "his word abiding in you."
- In verses 39-40 Jesus challenges their practice of appealing to the Torah (their scriptures) for their religious positions, and then he accuses them of not accepting that part of their scriptures that give supporting evidence about him.
- Verses 41-47 are summary statements by Jesus that he is not dependent on recognition from people to substantiate who he is and the validity of what he is doing. He chides his adversaries for being willing to accept the claims of people who have no support for their ego claims, but are so obtuse that they cannot, or will not, recognize the very working of God. Still, he says, he does not need to accuse them himself because their Torah (the writings of Moses) is witness for him against them. If they will not believe their own sacred writings, there is no reason to expect them to believe him.

> Keeping a focus on the unity of Father and Son is vital. Thinking of Father in heaven and Son on earth lends itself easily to separating them into different persons. Jesus always focuses on unity. John 8:42 and Philippians 2:6-7 are well translated, respectively: "I did not come on my own, but he sent me" (that is, we agreed on my coming); "though he (the Son) was in the form of God, he did not count equality with God a thing to be grasped [clung to], but emptied himself." While Jesus does not come in incarnation "on his own," neither is he sent "against his wishes."
>
> The reference to judging and judgment in verse 22 is not about end-time judgment. The Greek word is *krino* (to separate, make distinction, choose between). Verses 22-23 on the Son being able, having authority, being recognized as an authentic representative of divine truth. Only as people honor (hold in high esteem, believe worthy of trust) the Son as they do the Father (the Supreme God) will they heed his words and follow him.

...

In verses 25-29, Jesus makes what is probably his most basic statement about eternal destiny for human persons. Reference to "the dead" in verse 25 is about persons who are physically alive but "spiritually dead" in sin, but can still "hear the voice of the Son" and choose "the way of life." Those who are "in the tombs" is clearly a reference to those who have died physically. Beyond this physical life there is a certain correlation between the harmony or disharmony of our lives in relation to the character and values of God. If our lives are reconciled to synchronized harmony with God through trusting faith, spiritual new birth, and living commitment, then the outcome will be beatitude. Jesus declares that the opposite is (and will be) tragic. It is wise, then, to take seriously the words of Jesus: "repent and believe the gospel" (Mark 1:14-15).

...

THE FEEDING OF FIVE THOUSAND
(6:1-14)

All four gospels record a feeding of a multitude, but with variations that are quite understandable considering the different traditions behind the writing after a full generation of time (see also Matt. 14:13ff, Mark 6:31ff, Luke 9:10ff). John's gospel has Jesus going from Capernaum to Bethsaida, a distance of five or six miles to the east across the Jordan River as it empties into the Sea of Galilee. The site is described as a "lonely place" (*heremon* = desolate, deserted), apparently near Bethsaida but not in the city itself.

As is quite usual, a crowd follows Jesus and gathers around him. The question about how to provide food for the crowd leads to the outcome often described as "the multiplication of the loaves and fishes." The text records that Jesus takes "five loaves and two fish" (a lad's lunch), gives thanks, and has the food distributed to the crowd. All are fed and the leftovers are gathered, " . . . that nothing may be lost." The crowd is impressed by the "sign" they see in the event.

...

The traditional interpretation of this event is that Jesus miraculously "multiplies" the loaves and fishes to a sufficient amount to feed the crowd. The texts, however, do not describe the miraculous act. They report that all the people are fed. Another possibility has long been suggested and is widely accepted. Such a suggestion is fittingly appropriate in light of the culture of that time: the people who follow Jesus take food with them in anticipation of the need before returning home.

Sources of food are not readily present in the countryside. The fact that a lad has lunch supports the idea that such a custom is practiced. On the desert hillside among a large crowd, only an honest and open-hearted lad owns up to having any food. His example and the action of Jesus work a genuine miracle of warming hearts and turning "keepers" into "sharers," so there is more than enough for everyone. Each of us will believe the nature of the event as seems correct to us, but it is a "miracle" either way.

This "miracle" event, and the people's response in verses 14-15, make it appropriate to include some comment. The Fourth Gospel includes no record of John's baptism of Jesus, though John does speak of seeing "the Spirit descend as a dove" (1:32). Neither does this gospel record the "temptation" story of Jesus in the wilderness. These events help us to understand the events recorded here. In the wilderness Jesus declines to do three things:

1. *turn stones into bread to satisfy his hunger*
2. *jump unharmed off the temple wall*
3. *use political power to gain prominence and power in the world*

These three decisions by Jesus parallel three ways he chooses not to pursue his ministry of reconciliation. Jesus understands human nature well. He knows that if you give people what they want, they will take it gladly and want more (see John 6:26). But it will not change their relationship with God. Two times Jesus feeds crowds, but that is not how he seeks to reconcile people to God.

Jesus does many awe-inspiring things to meet human need. Crowds follow him as a wonder-worker and bring crowds of infirmed people to be healed, but physical health is not the same as spiritual wholeness. He heals to meet human need. Gathering a crowd is not his "mission." Jesus does not seek to enhance himself nor try to make people be good by ruling over them (see Luke 4:5-6, Mark 10:42-43). He consistently teaches that true greatness is in service, not prominence and controlling influence.

In the wilderness Jesus chooses what to do and what not to do in his incarnate ministry of reconciliation. If you "feed people, they will come." People will eat gift food, but it may well not make any change in their lives. If you do awe-inspiring "wonder works" such as jumping unharmed from a high wall, or healing people's physical infirmities, crowds will throng, seeking help or to "see a wonder." But that may not change the kind of persons they are. Control over people will not transform them. The Jewish religious authorities have controlled the people of Israel for a thousand years through required sacrifices, but that has not caused them to follow God faithfully. The occupying Romans control their lives but accomplish nothing more than to make the Jews hate them.

In the wilderness Jesus wisely knows that feeding people, overwhelming them with awe-inspiring "miracles," and controlling them with ritual requirements or political power will not change their hearts, transform their lives, and reconcile them to God. He leaves the wilderness and goes out to teach and preach a transforming message: "Repent and believe the gospel" (Mark 1:15). Jesus confirms the ancient inspiration of Micah that what God requires is not ritual sacrifices, but that people become the kind of people who "do justice, love kindness, and walk humbly with God" (6:8).

...

JESUS RESPONDS TO JEWISH MESSIANIC HOPES
(6:14-15)

The impression made by the feeding miracle stirs messianic hope among the crowd. Jesus senses the stirring and promptly goes away into the hills alone.

History lies behind the "people reaction" and needs to be understood in order to grasp the significance of John 6:14-15. After the Assyrians conquered the Northern Kingdom in 722 BCE, and the Babylonians conquered the Southern Kingdom and sacked the city of Jerusalem in 586 BCE, the "kingdom era" of Israelite history ended. The Israelites afterward lived under the dominance of other empires and dreamed of a time when an "anointed Son of David" would arise to be a messiah (an anointed one). One major stream of their hope was that the messianic king would be a great military leader, throw off the hated oppressors, and raise Israel to prominence and prosperity in a new golden age, as the days of David's reign had been. That messianic hope is openly manifest among the Jews in Palestine during the life and ministry of Jesus.

The Jews chafe under Roman occupation and hope for a delivering messiah. When Jesus does a "miracle" event, there stirs among the people anticipation that he may possibly be the fulfillment of that great hope. Such stirrings raise two problems for Jesus. He is aware that any "messianic demonstration" will call down on them harsh reaction by the Romans. Also note that Jesus keeps trying to help the people understand that he has not come to be that kind of messiah. His incarnate ministry is not about building the kingdom of Israel; it is about establishing the kingdom of God in the hearts and lives of people.

His ministry is to reconcile people to God, not create an earthly kingdom. The people do not understand him. They keep pursuing him, seeking to see "supernatural wonders." Jesus keeps patiently teaching them the "ways of the kingdom of God" until the Jewish leaders accomplish his death because he will not submit to their religious authority. In this instance, Jesus quietly goes away.

WALKING ON WATER
(6:16-21)

Three of the gospels provide accounts of Jesus walking on water, albeit with variations. Matthew (14:22-33) has the longest account and is the only one that includes Simon Peter's attempt to walk on water. Luke does not include the story at all. Mark (6:45-52) and John have shorter and more similar accounts.

It is night. Jesus has not returned to join the disciples. His followers start rowing from Bethsaida westward toward Capernaum. The sea is stormy. Jesus comes toward them "walking on the sea." He speaks to them, saying that it is he, and then joins them in the boat. Immediately they are on land.

The location and distances involved are important in trying to envision what might have happened. The disciples in the boat have left Bethsaida, or nearby, and are traveling west to Capernaum. Both towns are along the north shore of the Sea of Galilee, not more than 5 or 6 miles apart. There is no reason for them to venture far from shore, for that will increase the distance to row. The debated question about this story is whether Jesus walks on the water across the sea to the boat, or if Jesus walks along the shore and talks to the disciples on the nearby boat. Word study of the Greek does not answer that question for us.

All three gospel accounts include the identical wording *epi tes thalasses*. The question has to do with the meaning of *epi*, a preposition that varies in its meaning with the context. G. Abbot-Smith has two lexicon pages of explanations of New Testament references, and Walter Bauer has four pages of biblical and literary citations and explanations. The preposition is variously translated on, upon, at, by, before, towards, against, etc. The identical phrase is used in John 21:1 about an appearance by the risen Jesus to seven of the disciples on the shore of Galilee. There has been no question but that he is on the shore. We will each understand this passage as it has most meaning for us.

...

Asking whether we have here a supernatural phenomenon of a man walking on water poses the wrong question. The Eternal God who created the entire universe, with its physical natural laws, and raised up the human species, with life-determining moral laws, can do whatever God chooses—when, where, or how he chooses. It is never a question of what God can do. The right question is what God will do and why?

In the story before us, the disciples find themselves in a perilous situation. They are rowing a small fishing boat in the stormy sea in the night. The Sea of Galilee is noted for its quick-rising, turbulent storms.

I experienced this weather pattern firsthand when I co-hosted a tour group on a boat trip across the Sea of Galilee one sunny afternoon. The boat was much larger than the one the disciples used. It had a powerful diesel engine. In less time than it took us to cross the ten miles from Tiberias to Capernaum, one of the famous (infamous) Galilee storms swept down from the western mountains. It made the waters so turbulent that our boat could not dock at the pier until a sister boat created a quieter wake with its propellers and enabled our pilot to dock safely.

The important lesson in this story is about the distresses to which we are vulnerable when we are apart from God, and the peace that Jesus brings with the assurance of his presence and care. The disciples are obviously very near the shore: as soon as Jesus gets into the boat, they are at their destination.

...

MISSING JESUS
(6:22-26)

Some of the crowd stay overnight near Bethsaida, instead of returning to Capernaum in the late evening. Jesus has left them and gone away into the hills. The disciples have left in the boat without him. The next day they wonder where Jesus is. When some boats come in, the disciples go to Capernaum to search for Jesus. When they find him, they ask a curiosity question: "When did you come here?" Jesus answers with a revealing reply that should cause them to do some soul-searching: You didn't see the signs. You don't get the meaning of what happened. All it means to you is that you were fed. You come seeking a repeat today.

...

This incident, like so many during the ministry of Jesus, reflects the tendency of the people to be impressed by the wonder works Jesus does to meet human need. Their human reaction is to be pleased by those helpful deeds, to focus more on them than on his teaching, and to anticipate his repeating them. Jesus acts out of compassion to do kind and helpful things, but his primary focus is always on his ministry to reveal God and lead people to trust and reconciliation (Luke 4:42-44, Mark 1:14-15).

...

DIFFERENT KINDS OF BREAD
(6:27-34)

Jesus uses the people's interest in bread to teach a lesson about priorities, about what is most important in life, about how we let our values guide our choices and actions in life. He uses food to refer to what nourishes the body and to what nurtures the spirit. Breakfast is gone by lunch, but faith and hope and love endure. Referring to himself as the Son of Man, Jesus tells his hearers that enduring values are gifts of the spirit. God is the source of those gifts, and they are coming to the people through the incarnate Son. The people ask, in turn, about instructions for doing "the works of God." Jesus answers, "believe in him whom he (God) has sent." The people ask for a sign as proof of his religious authority. They cite the "bread" (manna) God provided through Moses. Jesus tells them the true bread is God's gift from heaven that gives life. The manna was temporary, "food that perishes." God's gift, the Son, has come to give life that is eternal. The people ask for the gift of "this bread."

...

In this conversation Jesus is helping the people distinguish between physical values and spiritual values. To understand this paragraph and the discourse that follows, keep in mind the use of metaphor. Material bread is easily understood as nourishment for the physical body. Bread as nurture for the spirit is a figurative use of metaphor. People often misunderstand this difference. Examples are the Samaritan woman in John 4:7-15 and the people in this passage. Jesus has to explain.

When Jesus tells the people that the "work of God" is "to believe," he does not spell out any rituals they are to perform. Having faith is a spiritual experience that may or may not lead to expression in physical action. The people in this incident want physical proof (a supernatural sign) to assure them of Jesus' religious authority.

The types of answers Jesus gives to questions of this kind is about people's freedom to choose faith and trust as the basis for having a relationship of harmony and living in reconciled unity with God. The conversation leads to the first of the "I AM" sayings and discourses recorded in John's gospel.

...

"I AM" THE BREAD OF LIFE
(6:35-40)

The people who have shared in the "multiplication" of the loaves and fishes the next day hear Jesus distinguish the true bread from heaven from the manna that the Hebrew ancestors ate in the wilderness. They ask Jesus to give them "this bread always." Jesus answers, "I Am the bread of life." He says that "whoever comes to him" shall not hunger, and "whoever believes in him" shall not thirst. He declares that he has come to do the Father's will, and that it is the will of the Father that everyone who believes in him (the Son) shall have eternal life.

This description by Jesus of himself as the bread of life, and that believing in him satisfies hunger and thirst, makes it clear that this is metaphor. His statement that the Father's will is that "whoever believes" shall have eternal life implies freedom of choice and affirms faith as the human response that leads to new birth in spiritual life. This is not about material bread, nor physical signs. This is about faith and trust in God.

This first "I AM" saying with following discourse introduces a distinctive feature of the Fourth Gospel. Jesus uses the phrase *ego eimi* (I AM). The word *ego* is the first personal pronoun of identification "I," and the word *eimi* is the first-person singular of the verb "to be" (I am). Used together they make the meaning emphatic, "I Myself Am," not some other person or thing.[1] A previous example is found in John 6:20 when Jesus speaks to assure the fearful disciples in the boat that "It is I Myself."

...

This use of the phrase I AM by Jesus, along with his consistent identification of himself as "the Son," leads to strong objection from Jewish religious leaders. They hear the I AM statement as the same as the divine name familiar from Exodus 3:13-14. His claim of sonship and unity with the Father is blasphemy to them. This sense of offense by the Jewish leaders is the central reason for their determination to eliminate Jesus, leading finally to his execution. His growing popularity with the crowds following him is also a threat to their positions of religious leadership and a cause for their animosity toward him.

...

JESUS AS BREAD FROM HEAVEN
(6:41-51)

The Jews are confused and offended at Jesus' words about having come down from heaven. After all they say, this is just a hometown man whose family we know. Jesus responds by saying he is fulfilling the promise of Isaiah 54:13 that "All your sons shall be taught by the Lord." He further affirms that he represents the Father; he is the one who knows the Father, for he has come from the Father. He says that whoever believes has eternal life. Calling himself "The living bread," he says that "the bread" he is giving "for the life of the world" is "my flesh."

Jesus claims for himself a status, as Son of the Father, that they do not believe. He declares that he has come for a purpose, to reveal the Father, that they do not recognize. He tells them that their ancient faith needs more adequate foundation. Those who ate manna died, because manna was physical food, and they (the crowd) need spiritual food about faith in God that he has come to reveal and make real for them.

EATING FLESH AND DRINKING BLOOD
(6:52-59)

Jesus calls himself the living bread, saying that whoever eats his flesh and drinks his blood "abides in me and I in him." He tells his hearers that his flesh is the bread that he will give for the life of the world. The Jews, referring to the Jewish leaders, continue to be confused about what Jesus means by "eating his flesh." Jesus describes his flesh as food and his blood as drink. He claims a mission from the Father to be "bread from heaven" that brings eternal life.

This is one of the most debated passages in the history of Christianity. The question has been about whether Jesus is describing literal cannibalism (eating human flesh). In the Jewish scriptures, eating the flesh of children is condemned as an idolatrous practice for Hebrews (Lev. 26:27-30). It is forecast to be practiced in cases of desperate survival (Deut. 28:52-57, 2 Kgs. 6:26-29, Jer. 19:7-9, Ezek. 5:8-10). Among the Israelites it is always a condemned practice based on their understanding that "the life is in the blood" (Gen. 9:4, Lev. 17:10-12, Deut. 12:23-24, 1 Sam. 14:33-34).

Religion in ancient Israel was practiced in a culture of pagan polytheism. Tribal religions believed that when an animal was sacrificed to a god, the spirit of the god entered the flesh of the animal. When a worshipper then ate the meat of that sacrificed animal, the consumer would eat the very god into their innermost being.[2] This practice in pagan religions is reflected in Paul's letter to Corinth (1 Cor. 8:4-10).

In early Christianity this question is still very real. The Lord's Supper (Eucharist) quotation "This is my body, . . . this is my blood of the new covenant" by the Christians leads to rumors among non-Christians that they are practicing cannibalism in their secret sacred meetings.[3]

…

Different branches of Christianity have developed different tenets of faith in understanding this passage and different meanings for their rituals practicing the Memorial Supper (Sacrament of Eucharist). No group has believed they are eating and drinking the physical flesh and blood of Jesus. Cannibalism is almost universally renounced. The physical body of Jesus has never been available. There have been three main streams of interpretation that underlie the denominational tenets and practices.

Transubstantiation, the Roman Catholic ritual sacrament, is the tenet and practice believed to be the actual practice of eating and drinking the "body and blood" of Jesus. In Catholic doctrine, transubstantiation means that when a correctly authorized priest elevates the elements of Eucharist during the Mass, God changes the "substance" of the elements from bread and wine to body and blood. The doctrine affirms that the "chemical composition" of the elements remains unchanged but the "substance" is entirely changed. (This doctrine was officially established by the Fourth Lateran Council in 1215 CE, and is the present doctrine based on the Council of Trent, Catechism # 1374, 1551 CE.[4])

This doctrine of "substance change" developed through centuries as the doctrine of "ritual sacraments" developed in the Christian movement. The problem of the church fathers is that they took the words of Jesus about eating his flesh and drinking his blood to be literal rather that symbolic. As such, they needed to find a way to have a "substance" present for the Eucharist.

Transubstantiation is a philosophical construct that enables a religious doctrine of divine change of the substance of bread and wine into the substance of body and blood of Jesus without changing the form and composition of the bread and wine. This is a faith tenet.

Consubstantiation is similar to but different from transubstantiation. In consubstantiation the body and blood of Jesus are "in, with, and under" the forms of bread and wine, but the form and substance of the bread and wine are not changed. This doctrine is often associated with Martin Luther. Some Lutherans do use the term, but Luther chose to use the term "sacramental union."[5]

John Calvin's view, called "spiritual presence," is very similar to Luther's "sacramental union" description. Calvin explained that in the Lord's Supper, either the Holy Spirit raises the church to communion with Christ in heaven or the Holy Spirit causes Christ to descend from heaven to commune with the church.[6]

Luther's doctrine of sacramental union and Calvin's doctrine of spiritual presence avoid the problem of requiring a literal substance presence at the Lord's Supper. Their tenets of faith maintain belief that the presence of Christ related to the elements of the Supper cause it to be a sacramental event conveying grace to the participant.

The "I Am" Revelations

The Free Church doctrine of the Memorial Supper is described by the Anabaptist Huldrych Zwingli (1484-1531 CE). According to Zwingli, the most important purpose of the Supper is Jesus' command to remember his sacrifice and reflect on what he has done for us through his death. For Zwingli, the elements of bread and wine are symbols whose purpose is to help us remember the "broken body" and "shed blood" of Jesus in the crucifixion.[7]

Zwingli's tenet accepts the symbolic meaning of the Supper, that its central purpose is memorial. His doctrine is specific that the memorial to be recalled and reflected on is the sacrifice of Jesus in crucifixion.

The traditional understanding of John 6:52-59 has focused on the statements about eating the living bread, about eating the flesh of Jesus and drinking his blood. That focus has led to traditions about the Lord's Supper, or more specifically belief about a sacramental miracle of bread and wine becoming body and blood in the Eucharist (Lord's Supper). This tenet of faith needs serious reconsideration.

In this discourse and throughout his many teachings, Jesus says that he has come from heaven, with the Father's "sending" and the Father's "blessing." Incarnation is pervasively central in understanding the life and teachings of Jesus. The writer of John's gospel cites the actions and teachings of Jesus as "signs" to reveal "who" Jesus is—the incarnate eternal Son of God. Jesus consistently says that the reason for his incarnate presence is to reveal God, and that believing in him and the Father will bring to life a quality of eternal life with God. Paul writes a truly inspired word to the Corinthians that "in Christ God was reconciling the world unto himself, not counting their trespasses against them" (2 Cor. 5:19). The redeeming work of Christ is the ministry of Jesus in the flesh (incarnation).

Jesus says, "the bread which I shall give for the life of the world is my flesh" (my incarnate life of ministry and teaching). Throughout this discourse and conversation, bread is figurative to symbolize the spiritual source of life with God that does not die. Eating is also figurative to symbolize the transforming dynamic of faith that bonds a person to God in eternal life. Jesus does not teach that any physical ritual, using any material elements, has a sacramental effect of bestowing the grace of God upon participants, or bonding the lives of participants to God. Rituals can have powerful meaning in our lives, but they only have meaning when an authentic experience of spiritual unity happens in our lives because of our response of faith and trust in God's works of grace.

In verse 40 Jesus summarizes that the will of God is for people to "see" (i.e. come to know the Son who reveals God) and to believe in him. He declares that to know and to have faith are the source of eternal life and the grounds for eternal hope.

Throughout this discourse by Jesus, references to "eating his flesh" and "drinking his blood" are metaphors meaning "to embrace the self-revelation of God's *character and purpose being made in the incarnation." Literal eating of his flesh and drinking his blood would have been impossible for them to do, and it would have been utterly abhorrent to the anti-cannibalism of their Jewish religion.*

The writer of the Fourth Gospel weaves this beautiful teaching and conversation together to show how this "sign" reveals who Jesus is and what is his mission in incarnation.

...

TESTED BY HIGH COMMITMENTS
(6:60-71)

Among the crowd following Jesus and hearing his teaching are some who call his words "a hard saying" (v. 60) that troubles them. Jesus responds by focusing on the distinction between the physical and spiritual dimensions of life: "the spirit gives life, the flesh is of no avail (profits nothing, counts for nothing"). He declares that he has been dealing with spiritual truths, and that spiritual enlightenment (granted by the Father) is vital for comprehending and responding favorably to spiritual truth. Many of his hearers respond by going away.

Jesus asks the Twelve if they are also going to desert him. As often happens, Simon Peter speaks for the group and affirms their faith in him, believing that Jesus is indeed teaching spiritual truth about life. They are convinced of that truth because of their faith that he has come from God. Jesus, in turn, warns them that challenges to come will test their loyalty and lead to treachery by one of them. The concluding verse is a summary by the writer after Judas is revealed as the betrayer.

...

The religious situation is becoming increasingly a time of crisis. The revelation Jesus is making by teaching and practice is so different from the faith and practices of Judaism that the people are confused and the Pharisees are convinced that Jesus is a blasphemer and false teacher. The Sanhedrin group is already determined to kill him (John 5:18, 7:1).

The crowds following Jesus are growing in number and enthusiasm. They are drawn to him by his wonder works (miracles), and many believe his teaching. They are confused, however, about "eating his flesh and drinking his blood." They do not grasp the figurative nature of "bread" as "spiritual truth" and "eating" as a metaphor for "believing." Their inability to understand leads to a testing time. Many simply leave. The Twelve declare that their faith in Jesus is firm: they are convinced of his authenticity as "the Holy One of God," and that there is no one else "to whom we shall go."

...

JEWISH OPPOSITION INCREASES
(7:1-13)

John 7 marks a transition in the ongoing ministry of Jesus. The adversarial relation between Jesus and the Jewish religious leaders is growing sharper. To reduce the likelihood of open conflict with Jewish religious leaders in Jerusalem, Jesus chooses to stay in Galilee and continue his teaching and ministry. His brothers, on the other hand, urge him to go to Jerusalem for a festival time, believing that to be a leader he must declare himself openly. John says in verse 5 that his brothers have not yet decided what to believe about Jesus. Are they trying to get him to reveal (expose) himself by forthright action?

Jesus tells them it is not the right time for him to make such a move, and then he urges them to go on to the feast. Their presence will not cause the same kind of stir that his presence would. The Jewish festival is significant to them in their heritage of religious experience.

Apart from the group and privately, Jesus does later go to Jerusalem. In Jerusalem there is active curiosity about whether he will come for the feast. Attitudes about Jesus are sharply divided. Their questions are not discussed openly because they do not want to get into trouble themselves with the authorities.

Jesus has a sensitive awareness about timing. He knows well the animosity of the Jerusalem power structure. The Sanhedrin rules the situation among the Jewish people. They are authorized and supported by the occupying Romans who require order. This Feast of Tabernacles is likely the one in the fall (early October) before the death of Jesus at Passover the following spring. The ministry of Jesus is at a watershed moment. The affirmation by Simon in verses 68-69, "You have the words of eternal life, and we have believed, and have come to know, that you are the Holy One from God," parallels in John the proclamation at Caesarea-Philippi that, "You are the Christ, the Son of the Living God" (Matt. 16:16). This commitment makes the situation vitally critical: the Twelve on the positive side versus the Jewish leadership seeking to annihilate Jesus.

Jesus is not ready to make the strategic move that is rapidly approaching. The parallel records of a healing in Matthew 17:14-18 and Luke 9:37-43, however, show that the time is near the end. Luke's record in 9:51 that Jesus "set his face to go to Jerusalem" indicates clearly that Jesus is moving through the days and events with an established purpose in mind.

...

Traditional understanding and interpretation of the focused purpose of Jesus is to go to the crucifixion and make a substitute expiatory blood sacrifice to pay the penalty for human sinfulness. That understanding is "read into" the Gospel accounts from sources other than the Gospels.

> Jesus does not teach nor act as if that is his incarnate purpose in life. He does not reveal the character of the Father as a God of justice, requiring the scales of morality to be equalized by penalty to match the evil before forgiveness can be given and harmony restored. Jesus reveals the Father as a God of mercy, whose loving concern is the repentant conversion and commitment of trust from us so that harmony and reconciliation prevail between us.
>
> This variance in belief about the character of God has led through the centuries to divergences in the tenets of faith about the Incarnation, the Crucifixion, and the doctrines of salvation. These differences are reflected in the remainder of this study of John.

...

TEACHING AND CONTROVERSY
(7:14-36)

At a time when the Temple is crowded with pilgrims who have come to the Feast, Jesus goes to the Temple and teaches. The religious authorities are puzzled by Jesus' teaching for two reasons. They wonder why he dares to teach in the Temple because he has not been properly authorized to do so. They consider him "unlearned"—he has not been trained in the priestly and rabbinical schools. They are, however, also surprised at the insight and wisdom of his teaching.

Jesus responds that he is teaching truth from God and that anyone who really wants to know truth will recognize it. In the ongoing conversation Jesus demonstrates the weakness in the claims of the Jewish leaders. He uses the teaching of Moses and the sabbath circumcision practices of the Jews to illustrate for them the way they rationalize about the Sabbath. The reference to a "deed (work)" in verse 21 is a carryover from ongoing controversy. The issue in their controversy is about Sabbath healing or Sabbath violation. The last previous record of sabbath healing is during a previous visit to Jerusalem (see 5:1-16). No healing is recorded during this visit. Jesus declares as valid principle that healing an invalid person is as equally an appropriate thing to do on a sabbath as performing a ritual circumcision.

People in the crowd are confused. They are well aware of the opposition of the religious authorities, so they are amazed that Jesus is teaching openly in the Temple. They recognize the boldness and wisdom of Jesus, but they are puzzled because his heritage is well known. "Hometown man" and "Messiah" are totally contradictory ideas for them. It is a part of the Jewish messianic hope that the heritage of the Messiah will not be known.

The Jewish authorities try to find a way to arrest Jesus without stirring tumult among the people. The statement by Jesus about going "where they cannot find him nor follow him" is about the ending of the Incarnation. It leaves the Jewish leaders bewildered.

PROMISE OF LIVING WATER
(7:37–8:1)

On the high holy day of the feast, Jesus proclaims an invitation to the crowd. His message is the same that he made to the Samaritan woman at Sychar (John 4:13-14): the thirsty can be refreshed by the truth he is teaching, and faith in him will be living waters of Holy Spirit. (Verse 39 is commentary by the writer looking back after the Crucifixion, Resurrection, and Pentecost.) The message of Jesus is convincing to some who are able to believe he is indeed the Messiah. Others are confused because they identify him with Nazareth where he has grown up instead of his ancestral birthplace in Bethlehem. The people are divided, but not clearly enough to enable the officers to arrest him.

When the officers report back to their superiors (v. 32), a division develops among the authorities also. The Pharisees demand action, but Nicodemus insists that they follow proper procedures. They turn their attack on Nicodemus. The time of turmoil ends with the people going home and Jesus retreating to the Mount of Olives.

JESUS, THE FORGIVER
(8:2-11)

The interchange in the Temple ends when the crowds leave the Temple at the end of the day, the concluding day of the Feast. Jesus does not leave the area, however, and will take up his teaching again, presumably in the Temple (see verse 20). The writer of John's gospel includes here a passage that has a questioned textual history. The event described is not present in any of the most reliable early manuscripts, and the early church fathers do not provide commentary on it. This textual history seems to indicate that it lived in oral tradition for some time and a later copyist inserted it. We can well agree that the story is so characteristic of the way Jesus deals with people and responds to his adversaries that our knowledge of him is enriched by its textual preservation.

The event is enlightening. The Pharisees are apparently gleeful that they have an incident they can use to entrap and discredit Jesus. They have a woman caught in adultery. An ancient Hebrew law going back to Moses condemns adulterers, men and women, to death by stoning (Deut. 22:13-24), or later in the Mishnah by strangulation.

The Pharisees confront Jesus with a request for his judgment. Instead of answering immediately, Jesus bends down and writes on the ground, apparently reflecting on his response. At their prodding he rises and says, "Let him who is without sin among you be the first to throw a stone at her." Then he bends back down and continues writing.

There is no record of what Jesus wrote, but as he usually does, Jesus gives them a response that causes them to know the answer to their own question. The accusers quietly go away. When the woman tells Jesus that none of the accusers is still present to condemn her, he answers, "Neither do I condemn you; go, and do not sin again."

> We do not know the circumstances of this guilty woman, but we do know about the status of women in ancient Jewish culture. Girls were considered to belong to their father or oldest brother until they married. After marriage they belonged to their husbands. Old Testament descriptions reveal that girls and women were treated as chattel property, a level above slaves or cattle. Biblical stories reveal clearly that within the family many wives, daughters, and sisters were richly treasured and treated with love and kindness. But women who did not have a male protector and provider were most often reduced to begging or prostitution for survival. That may well be the situation for the woman in this story.
>
> Take note that the Pharisees do not bring for judgment the guilty man. They tell Jesus that the woman has been caught in the act, so they surely know who the guilty man is. The text reveals their motivation. They are usually very zealous to enforce every detail of their religious laws, but in this case the woman is to them a pawn in their determination to destroy Jesus.

...

The incident reveals how different Jesus is from the Pharisees, who believe themselves to be and are believed by Jews generally to be the most faithful followers of Moses. But they are very harsh and in no sense compassionate toward wretched people who are less than totally committed to every ritual detail of Mosaic law as the Pharisees interpret it. Jesus, by contrast, is committed to redeeming people's lives in every way possible.

One of the tragic features of so much religion throughout human history is the tendency of zealous religionists to cast off and condemn to perdition any who do not "walk their approved line." Jesus, and those who understand God best, are committed to include and strive for the recovery, renewal, and enhanced life of broken and fallen fellow humans. Jesus does not approve of the woman's sinful life. While he does not condemn her, he tells her to not go on sinning.

...

I AM THE LIGHT
(8:12-20)

John 8 contains the second of the I AM discourses in the gospel. Jesus says, "I AM the light of the world." He restates the great proclamation the writer sets forth in the prologue that the Word (*Logos*) shares with God in the eternal essence of life and in the origin of all creation. He further declares that the life in the Logos that became flesh and dwells among us is the source of light for mankind, light that darkness cannot "swallow up" and "put out."

Jesus claims through his words that, since he is the light of the world, to follow him is to walk in the light; to be able to see and recognize and avoid the tragic false ways of darkness. His proclamation offends the Pharisees because his teaching is so often different from theirs that is based on the traditions they have "received from Moses and the elders." They accuse Jesus of teaching false and blasphemous things that have no supporting authority because he is making the claims on his own and has no Torah teaching to back him up. Jesus replies in response that he does not need supporting authority because he has a source of knowledge different from and superior to theirs.

Citing the Torah that the witness of two persons is sufficient to support a testimony, he claims the support of the Father and himself for the validity of what he is saying. They throw back at him: "Where is this Father" that you claim has sent you? Jesus exposes their lack of informed spiritual insight by declaring that they do not comprehend who "He and the Father" are and what is their relationship. The writer pens a concluding description of this conversation to show that the religious leaders do not understand the meaning of the "signs" in what Jesus teaches and does that reveal who he really is. The Pharisees oppose his teaching and are angered that he is teaching in the Temple, but they can find no way to get him arrested.

GROWING DIFFERENCES
(8:21-30)

An ongoing conversation follows from the questions raised when Jesus describes himself as being the light of the world. Jesus makes a statement, strange to the Pharisees, that he will go away, they cannot follow, and they will die in their sin. They wonder if he means that he will kill himself. Jesus replies that the difference is that they are of this world and he is not. Their confusion about who Jesus really is leads to statements by Jesus about the relationship between himself and the Father. To speak further to their confusion, Jesus declares that when he is "lifted up" they will understand better the unity of relationship and action between him and the Father.

The words of Jesus about "going away" are references to the approaching end of the Incarnation, the end of his physical ministry, and his return to the realm of spirit from whence he has come. The Pharisees cannot comprehend what he is saying. Their religious understanding is based on Judaism, a religion of rituals and sacrifices. The teachings and actions of Jesus are revealing a different character of God and meaning of religion. The Pharisees do not believe that Jesus reveals God and teaches correctly. Jesus forthrightly claims the unity between himself and the Father, which his opposers just as forthrightly deny. There is no acceptance by them or harmony between them. The writer records, however, that many do believe in Jesus.

...

Two parts of this passage need comment. One has to do with the conversation by Jesus about the relationship with the Father. Any conversation about God as Father/Son/Holy Spirit reveals the inadequacy of our human ability to think and describe. Jesus always emphasizes the unity between himself and the Father. Human words and descriptions "sound like" two persons. Our problem is that the concept of two persons (two separate individuals) really means two gods.

The word triunity has been for centuries the defined tenet about Father/Son/Holy Spirit. Triunity, however, is a hybrid word created to describe a relationship whose awesome mystery we can neither comprehend nor describe. Triunity is an oxymoron; each part of it is contradictory in contrast to the other. Three is not one, and one is not three. One person can have three facets of selfhood, but not be three persons. We need to follow Jesus and make sure we keep the oneness of God central to our faith.

A second statement in the passage needs comment. Jesus refers to the Son of Man being "lifted up." This statement is traditionally interpreted to mean "hung on a cross" as a substitute sacrifice. Context in the Fourth Gospel is different. In John 3:14 the "lifting up" of the Son of Man is set as a parallel in meaning with the lifting up of a serpent in the wilderness (Num. 21:9). The serpent in the wilderness was "lifted up" as an object to help the people have faith in God, not as a substitute sacrifice to bear the penalty of disobedience by the people. In the Gospels, Jesus is revealed as the incarnate Son who is to be "lifted up" (proclaimed) and "believed in" and trusted by faith; a Son who has come from the Father to bring light and truth, grace and mercy, for humankind.

...

"ABRAHAM'S CHILDREN"
(8:31-40)

The interchange that took place in Jerusalem during a Feast of Tabernacles in September/October (see 7:2-14, 19-23) continues in John 8. A question about authentic discipleship arises when Jesus declares that true disciples are those who believe in him, know the truth, and are made free by it. In verses 30-31 the text describes Jesus as talking with those believing Jews. No explanation is given about the difference that follows. The Jews claim that heritage from Abraham gives them cherished status and deny that they have ever been in bondage. Jesus turns the discussion to sinfulness: "Everyone who commits sin is a slave to sin" (v. 34).

In verses 37-38 Jesus declares that he is revealing and teaching truths about the character and intentions of God that are different from the traditions the Jews have learned to believe and practice in their religious heritage. They repeat the claim that they are Abraham's children. Jesus uses the great tradition that Abraham was a "man of faith." He applies spiritual and moral character and action instead of physical ancestry, and refutes their claim to being Abraham's children because they are not doing what Abraham did.

The Jews claim that as Abraham's children they have never been in bondage to anyone. This ignores their ancestral heritage. Their sacred documents detail both Egyptian bondage and Babylonian exile. Jesus, in turn, declares that true freedom is to be made free by truth.

...

The issue here is the same as Henry van Dyke claims in his poem "Home Song" that "Stone walls do not a prison make, Nor iron bars a cage." Does "bondage" have to do with restraints on physical life or with blights on life by immoral conduct and spiritual distortions? Does freedom have to do with freedom of physical movement or with freedom of soul through forgiveness and peace?

...

LIVING BY DIFFERENT HERITAGES
(8:41-47)

The claim by Jesus to have come from God is answered with the accusation that "We were not born of fornication," apparently denying his "virgin birth" that must have been "voiced abroad" in the Jerusalem area. Jesus, in turn, makes clear claim of his incarnate status, and declares that a true relationship with God comes by recognizing him as an authentic revealer of God's truth. He declares straightforwardly to them that the reason they do not hear God's truth in his words is that they are not "of God"—that is, they are not in harmony with God through their religious traditions and practices. They are not true children of Abraham.

Jesus and the Jewish leaders are contending that they have come from different heritages—he from God directly, and they from God through Abraham. Jesus refutes their claim that their heritage from Abraham takes them to God. He charges that they are so unfaithful to the heritage of Abraham that they are no longer true children of Abraham. He accuses them of living in a heritage of evil as though the devil is their father.

...

Jesus is using language that belonged to one developing period of human understanding about the source of evil. Throughout the historical eras before the Babylonian Captivity, humanity believed that good and evil came from the same source (moral monism). Good happened if the deity (God/god) to whom someone belonged was pleased with their obedience and homage. Bad (evil) happened if their deity was displeased and was chastising them. As people came to believe in one supreme deity (monotheism), their understanding of evil also developed as moral dualism (good and evil having their origin in separate sources).

This change occurred during the historical timeframe of the Babylonian Captivity (after about 600 BC). In both Persian Zoroastrianism and Babylonian/post-Babylonian Judaism, there developed the belief that good had its origin in God, and evil had its source in a less-than-divine demigod. The believed-in demigod was variously named Angra Mainyu (Evil Spirit), or later Shaitan by the Zoroastrians,[8] and Satan (adversary) by Jews and Christians. A new—and I am convinced a more accurate—doctrine of evil began to also emerge in post-Babylonian Judaism as the documents of the Hebrew Sacred Scriptures took organized written form.

The creation stories and the parable of the Garden of Eden in the beginning of Genesis reflect belief in human nature as characterized by the capacity to make moral choice and have freedom of choice as divinely designed and endowed gifts. Temptation can still come from a "Tempter" (something or someone outside a person), but evil results from moral choices made by "the woman" (Eve) and "the man" (Adam). (See also Micah 6:6-8.)

In the later Christian era, belief about evil continued to develop until an inspired awareness came to be written in the brief document titled the Letter of James. *"Each person is tempted when he is lured and enticed by his own desire" (see James 1:13-15).*

In John 8, Jesus declares that the Jews have so chosen to alter and refocus the meaning and practices of their religion that their heritage is no longer a true heritage from Abraham. They are no longer "doing what Abraham did."

...

CONCLUDING CONFRONTATION
(8:48-59)

The Jewish denial of Jesus' authenticity continues with a charge that he is a Samaritan (not a true Israelite) and that he is demon possessed. Jesus continues to state his true representation of God and declares that "his word" (the truth of his teaching) is the key to life victorious over death.

Much of what happens in this extended interchange is adversarial "give and take" between Jesus and the Jews. With their example that Abraham and all the prophets died, they challenge his words about not being subject to death. They are claiming Abraham as their greatest authority, and Jesus says that he has superior status through his unity with the Father and his eternal deity, "before Abraham was, I AM."

...

The controversy has become harsh. The Jews are deeply offended by Jesus. They have heard all they are willing to hear. When they cannot discredit him, in Jewish custom they take up stones to stone him. Jesus evades them and leaves the Temple, but he stays in the city for some additional time.

...

A BLIND MAN HEALED
(9:1-12)

All of John 9 records an incident of healing and the controversy that follows it. Jesus does what he so often did: He meets a human need and helps a person. The man has been blind from birth. Developed medical science and knowledge of genetic inheritance are far in the future. Common belief is that illness and physical handicaps are a result of and punishment for sinfulness. His disciples ask Jesus if the man's blindness is caused by him or his parents. Jesus answers, "Neither." Meeting human need is a work he has come to do in the world, and healing this blind man will demonstrate the caring compassion of God. In this instance Jesus anoints the man's eyes with clay and sends him to wash in the pool of Siloam. After the healed man moves about with vision, some people wonder whether it is really the same man. He says freely that he is the man, and when questioned about how his sight came to him, he tells them. He knows and tells them his healer was Jesus, but he does not know where Jesus now is.

SABBATH CONTROVERSY AGAIN
(9:13-17)

The healing of the blind man happens on a Sabbath. When it is reported to the Pharisees, they go into action. They question the man about how he is healed and who did it. The healed man readily describes his healing. The Jews make their usual response, i.e., this can't have anything to do with God since this man violates the sanctity of the Sabbath like this. Some people in the crowd respond with a "how can this be?" reaction: "How can a person who is a sinner" do something like this "that looks so much like God at work?" This simple observation leaves the Pharisees without an answer. They ask the healed man what he thinks of Jesus, and the healed man replies that he is a prophet.

TRYING TO SOLVE A DILEMMA
(9:18-34)

The baffled Jews do not believe an authentic healing has taken place until they question his parents. The parents do not want to get involved because it is clearly known that anyone who admits to believing Jesus is the Messiah will be expelled from the synagogue. The parents evade by replying, "Ask him." After a repeat of their questioning him, the healed man replies with incredulity: "You are religious leaders who are supposed to know about religious things, and you don't know that no one but God can give sight to someone born blind?" In response, since they cannot refute his challenge, in frustration they do the only thing they know to do: they expel him from the synagogue.

...

If you can't solve a problem, simply deny it and try to get rid of it. That's not a good approach to problems.

...

FOLLOW-UP HELP AND WARNING
(9:35-41)

Jesus later finds the healed man and identifies himself to him as his benefactor and as the Son of Man. The healed man expresses faith and homage. Jesus goes on to declare that his presence in the world will enable some to see (have insight) while others will become "blind" when introduced to spiritual light and truth. In spite of their opportunity to see light and hear truth, some will reject both and choose to continue in their blindness. Jesus makes a concluding declaration: they will bear responsibility for their choices—"your guilt remains."

The Pharisees are always following Jesus, trying to trap and discredit him. Some of them heard what Jesus said about people being blind. They accost Jesus again, scoffing with the question, "Are you really saying that we are blind?" Jesus replies that by pretending to see, they prove themselves guilty of "spiritual" blindness.

...

Underlying this controversy about "blindness" is the matter of discerning what is believed to be true and who is the authentic authority to trust about what is truth.

The developed history of evolving human concepts about the nature and character of God, and the meaning and purpose of religion, illustrates the principle of "incremental learning." Humanity has progressively "learned" about natural laws, the physical universe, human physiology, genetic coding, and other factual information. Human beliefs about deity have evolved from tribal polytheism to universal monotheism. Religious tenets have developed on the basis of both fear and love. Some people believe that God is first of all a God of justice, requiring the scales to be leveled. Others believe that God is a God of mercy and grace, focusing on reconciliation through repentant faith and forgiveness.

For anyone who believes Jesus of Nazareth is the incarnate revelation of the nature, character, and will of God, his life and teaching are the truth that brings the light of life for human persons.

...

A DISCOURSE ABOUT SHEPHERDING
(10:1-13)

Jesus uses the example of sheep and shepherd, and the relationship between them, to teach about the relationship between himself and the people. Two "I Am" sayings are included: "I Am the Door of the sheep," and "I Am the Good Shepherd." He begins with examples of shepherds and thieves, those who belong with the sheep and those who do not, those who care for the sheep and those who want to "take from" the sheep. He says that the sheep know the difference, but they need the protection of the gatekeeper who will let in only the true shepherds.

Jesus describes himself as the true gatekeeper, the "door of the sheep," the true entry into the sheepfold of God. His coming is to bring abundant life, not to steal from and destroy. For this mission he will "lay down his life" (invest his incarnate life protecting his followers from false teachers and nurturing them with truth). Jesus says that he knows his own and his own know him.

The life and role of shepherding are prominent in the economy of first-century Palestine. Shepherds tend their own flocks, spend much of their lives with the sheep, know them so individually that they give them names, lead them to grazing, and secure them in safe places at night. Some owners do hire men to tend their flocks.

Jesus uses the difference between owner-shepherds and hired tenders-of-sheep to describe the difference he has with people who learn to trust and follow him. An obvious reference behind this teaching is that there are other "teachers" (Jewish leaders) whose "voices" (teachings) are so different from his that those who recognize his "voice" find their "voices" strange and will not follow them. Jesus continues in a discourse to explain.

JESUS AS THE GOOD SHEPHERD
(10:14-18)

Jesus makes a contrast between himself and "hirelings." This is an evident reference to the Jewish religious leaders who are dogging his steps and harshly opposing his teachings and his influence on the crowds who gather around him everywhere he goes. Jesus declares himself to be the "good shepherd." He leaves no doubt by using the emphatic phrase "I AM (I MYSELF AM) the Good Shepherd."

Jesus expands his declaration with a description of the unity that exists between his followers, himself, and the Father. He deepens the meaning of this unity by declaring again that he will "lay down his life" for the sheep. In verse 11 he describes a true shepherd as one who has such commitment to and such care for his sheep that he will lay down (spend, invest) his life to lead them to green pastures and protect his flock with rod and staff (Ps. 23:2, 4). In this paragraph he declares that as the Good Shepherd he will indeed lay down his life for the sheep.

Jesus says that he has other sheep, "not of this fold." He declares a mission to bring them into the "one flock" with "one shepherd."

…

The statements by Jesus in verses 17-18 are both prescient and contextual. Throughout his public ministry Jesus has focused on teaching, helping, and reconciling—the broad scope of God's total incarnate purpose. The writer of John's gospel makes wide use of metaphor to convey the meaning of Jesus' actions and teachings. I find the statements here about laying down his life to be more in accord with Paul's admonition to "present your bodies as a living sacrifice (of service) (Rom. 12:1) more than about foretelling a death as "substitute atoning blood sacrifice." The Incarnation itself is always reflected by Jesus as an "investment" by God.

The words of Jesus in verse 18 that he has "power" to lay down and to take up are revealing. The Greek is exousian *(right to do, authority to do, and ability to do), not* dunamis *(power to do). It seems clear that for Jesus both incarnation and crucifixion are voluntary. It is God's choice to make self-revelation through incarnation. It is Jesus' choice to lay down (spend, invest) his incarnate life in teaching and ministry.*

His living revelation of God's character and reconciling outreach has led to strong disagreement, harsh offense, and planned violent reaction among Jewish religious leaders (I think of it as the consequence of incarnation). At this time Jesus is indeed referring to the "end events" of his physical life.

By voluntary and deliberate intent, Jesus is on his way to Jerusalem to literally lay his life on the line. He has taught that true greatness is in service. In Jerusalem he will challenge arrogant and corrupt power. Arrogant, corrupt, powerful men will accomplish his execution. Jesus will live and reveal forever that human earthly power is vanquished by life in God's grace. The events and teachings recorded here occur just before all of the happenings of Passion Week. Jesus has "set his face" to go to Jerusalem (Luke 9:51), and he is now nearing that city and that time.

...

THE DIVIDED JEWS
(10:19-21)

The discourse about being the Good Shepherd causes the usual confusion and disagreement in the Jewish crowd. Some in the group claim that Jesus is surely demon-possessed and blasphemous. Others are convinced that a demon-possessed person surely cannot restore sight to the blind and teach such caring and helpful truths. Unreconcilable viewpoints create the horns of a dilemma for them.

DURING A FEAST OF DEDICATION
(10:22-42)

Jesus is in Jerusalem in the Temple area. The people question, "Are you really the Messiah?" Jesus chooses to not answer "Yes" or "No." His answer here is like his answer to the disciples of John the Baptist: "Go and tell John what you have seen and heard" (Luke 7:22). This is the same sense that the writer of the Fourth Gospel uses the figure of "signs" to describe actions of Jesus as indications of who he is and what he is doing. Jesus tells the Jewish crowd that his actions are a witness to who he is. His critics, however, do not recognize him because they are "not his sheep." They are not people who have come to trust him and follow him. He again declares the unity between himself and the Father, and the grace of caring that will sustain those who are his sheep, who do trust and follow him.

The contentious interchange threatens violence as his adversaries take up stones to kill Jesus. He does not recoil from their threats. He simply asks why they want to kill him. They reply that it is not for any good work that he has done, but for the blasphemy they believe he is committing by claiming to be the Son of God. Jesus quotes Psalm 82:6 to remind them that all of God's people are called sons of God. He tells them to take note of what he is doing and how that is a witness that he is truly representing God. They turn from threatening to stone him to try to arrest him, but he escapes them and leaves Jerusalem. He goes away across the Jordan valley and stays a while. Crowds follow him, and many people believe in him.

A place-of-ministry question arises in this section, with several variations noted:

- John 7:2 locates Jesus in Jerusalem during a Feast of Tabernacles (about October 1).
- In John 8:2 and 9:7 the places noted are still in Jerusalem.
- All of chapter 9 is about a single event in Jerusalem.
- John 10:19-21 describes the people being divided over the healing of a blind man, which is the incident recorded in chapter 9.
- John 10:22 locates Jesus in Jerusalem during a Feast of Dedication (about December 1).
- There is no record of Jesus leaving Jerusalem from John 7:22–10:39.
- Some of the events in this section of Luke's travel record (Luke 9:51–13:21) describe events away from Jerusalem.

The records do not readily harmonize, but differences in time-and-place records do not affect the validity of the events and teachings. It is interesting to note, however, that if Jesus stayed in Jerusalem for two months among the adversarial Jewish leaders without leaving the city, it reflects a significant variation from his more usual itinerant pattern of movement.

THE RAISING OF LAZARUS
(11:1-44)

John 11 records the "raising of Lazarus" and another of the "I AM" sayings. The "Lazarus" family members in Bethany are close personal friends of Jesus (see Luke 10:38-42). Lazarus is very sick. His sisters, Mary and Martha, send word to Jesus about his being ill. Jesus is some distance away from Bethany (John 10:40) and does not come immediately. He waits two days before starting his journey (John 11:6). When he arrives in Bethany, Lazarus has been entombed for four days (John 11:17). Jesus seems to imply (see v. 4) that he purposely delayed in going until after Lazarus died.

When Jesus tells the disciples they will go to Judea, the disciples remind him of the threat to his life if he goes there. Jesus replies that Lazarus has died, so they will go to "awaken" him. The disciples don't understand as Jesus talks interchangeably about "sleep" and death. Jesus finally says plainly, "Lazarus is dead." The disciples agree among themselves to go with Jesus in spite of the danger involved.

When they arrive in Bethany, Martha goes to meet Jesus and laments to him that if he had come earlier he could have kept her brother from dying. She declares her faith, however, that Lazarus can be made alive again because God will grant such a request if Jesus asks him. Jesus tells her that Lazarus will rise again, but she understands that to mean a resurrection at the end of time. It is in answer to her statement that Jesus says, "I AM the resurrection and the life." Jesus asks Martha if she believes that, and she

The "I Am" Revelations

replies that she believes he is the Messiah. She affirms that she can trust the truthfulness of what he has said.

Martha goes and tells Mary that Jesus has arrived and is asking for her. Mary goes out to meet Jesus, and the gathered friends follow her, assuming she is going to the tomb. Mary also laments to Jesus that he has not come in time to keep Lazarus from dying. They go to the tomb, and there Jesus weeps, joining the sisters and friends in their grief.

Jesus tells them to remove the stone from the mouth of the cave tomb. Martha responds that the body is already beginning to decay. The situation seems hopeless to her. Jesus instructs them and they do remove the stone. He prays to assure the people that what is about to happen is the work of God. Then he calls Lazarus and Lazarus comes forth in graveclothes wrappings. Jesus tells those nearby to free him. This incident stands in the Christian tradition as an assurance that life triumphs over death through the grace and power of God.

Jewish funeral practice calls for purifying and preparing a body and burying it as soon as possible after death,[9] as they believe the soul is disoriented after the death of the body. One source writes that for the first twelve months the soul hovers over the body.[10] William Barclay cites a tradition in harmony with this passage that the soul hovers near the body for four days in hope of reunion with the body.[11]

The declaration by Jesus that he is "the resurrection and the life" has become one of the central anchors of the Christian faith. Death is not the "end" for those who believe in Jesus. His ongoing explanation in the passage reflects the twofold meaning of death as the word is used here. The statement is made more easily understood by a simple amplification: "He who believes in me, though he die (physically), yet shall he live (spiritually), and whoever lives (physically) and believes in me shall never die (spiritually)."

...

The raising of Lazarus is the only record in John of Jesus raising a dead person to life, whereas two are recorded in the Synoptics. This account is the only one of the three that tells of a "raising" at a time later than very shortly after death. We are simply unable to imagine how to think about these three stories. They are written as records of physical body resuscitations. The descriptions are of physical bodies coming back to life as if they had not died. The assumption is left, but not stated, that the three individuals resume normal physical life. Lazarus is the only one mentioned again later in the text. He is described as being present at dinner, and being a "person of interest" (Luke 12:2, 9).

We know about the deterioration processes that begin immediately after death, all of which would have to be reversed for the body to be alive again. It is widely believed that instances of "near time" recovery such as the son of the widow of Nain (Luke 7:11-15), and of the daughter of Jairus (Matt. 9:23-26, Mark 5:35-43, Luke 8:49-56) were "near death" recoveries whose stories were expanded over time to enhance their wonder and impact. The "raising" of Lazarus is a different situation.

William Barclay writes that "we are in the end compelled to say that we do not know what happened at Bethany,"[12] but that "something tremendous did happen." Wilbert Howard concludes that "it is useless to ask what was the event in the early tradition that John has adapted and retold in his own way and for the purpose declared in John 20:31."[13] The purpose may well be to adapt a traditional story to provide a setting for and to illustrate the saying, "I AM the resurrection and the life." Wilbert Howard writes further, "The dominant thought throughout the narrative (and I add, the entire Fourth Gospel) is that Jesus is the life essential and eternal . . . and such life . . . becomes a present possession where Jesus is."[14]

As for me, I believe there were actual happenings behind more of the gospel event stories than some writers say are simply made-up stories to make points. It does seem evident that many of the "events" are expanded, even exaggerated, in the texts as we have them. About the "miracle" nature of the wonder works of Jesus, it is never a question for me about what God can do. My question is always what will God do and what did God do?

The purpose for the Incarnation was not to solve every humanly unsolvable problem nor to meet every human physical need. Jesus compassionately responded to human needs when he met them as he went about his mission, living and teaching, revealing the character of God as loving and merciful, and reconciling trusting sinners into forgiven persons in harmony with God.

. . .

AGAIN, DIVIDED REACTIONS
(11:45-53)

Many witnesses to the work of Jesus are convinced and believe in him. Some go to the Jewish authorities and report what Jesus has done. The Sanhedrin Council is convened to consider what to do. Caiaphas, the high priest for the year (and a chief member of the Sanhedrin), speaks up. He does a rude put-down of others who are hesitant to take radical action. His proposal is to get Jesus killed to remove both their religious problem and the political peril from the nation.

Verses 51-52 are an interpretive comment by the writer of this record. Verse 53 records that the raising of Lazarus is a "last straw" for the members of the Sanhedrin. Henceforth they are determined that Jesus must die.

The Jewish religious leaders always have two concerns about Jesus. They believe him to be a blasphemer for acting as a representative of God when they know he has grown up in Nazareth, he is not an approved rabbi, and his teachings are not in accord with the established teachings of the traditional Jewish faith. They are also concerned about his popularity with the masses.

The Roman Empire dominates that part of the world, occupies it with military forces, and allows Jewish leaders to manage civil and religious affairs as long as they maintain order and the required taxes are collected. Any civil disorder is a matter of harsh reaction by the Roman authorities. The concern of the Sanhedrin is that those following Jesus will become so large a crowd that the Romans will consider it dangerous as a revolutionary religious movement, wipe it out, destroy their temple, and take away their governing privileges.

A few words about the relationship of Caiaphas and Annas, who are both described as influential leaders of the Sanhedrin in the gospel records of the trials of Jesus: Annas is the father-in-law of Caiaphas and something of a "power behind the throne." The Jews consider the position of chief priest as a hereditary role for life. They would prefer Annas to still be chief priest. The Romans, however, require that the office of chief priest change at their choosing to prevent any one man from becoming powerful enough to create insurgent problems.[15]

In Jewish belief of that era a high priest is often a prophetic spokesman for God to declare things he does not know. From the writer's perspective, and from the tradition that developed among the Christians before the writing of John, Caiaphas believes that the death of Jesus will prevent Roman reaction to a possible messianic insurrection. And, though he does not realize it, Caiaphas prophesies (vv. 51-52) that the death of Jesus will secure the nation from "present" destruction by the Romans and sustain the nation for the messianic hope of gathering the "scattered children of God" home to their "promised land" again.

JESUS CHOOSES HIS TIMING
(11:54-57)

The text does not indicate that Jesus becomes aware of the extent of radical determination by the Jewish authorities to silence him, but he knows that he can no longer do ministry in the region of Jerusalem without constant harassing opposition from them. Ephraim is a few miles north of Jerusalem, across the border between Judea and Samaria, so Jesus goes there with his disciples and stays for a while.

Winter is giving way to spring, and the momentous season of Passover is coming soon. Pilgrims are already arriving from across the nation to "purify themselves" in preparation for participating in the rituals of the great feast.

Their interest in Jesus does not grow quiet just because he is away from the city. There is lively talk about him and wondering by the people whether he will come to Jerusalem during the Passover celebration. The Jewish leaders do not intend to let their guard down. They mean to arrest him, and so they order anyone who knows of his whereabouts to inform them. The stage is set for one of the most significant weeks in human history. Holy Week is at hand.

NOTES

[1] William F. Arndt and F. Wilbur Gingrich, eds., *Walter Bauer's, Greek-English Lexicon of the New Testament, 2nd ed.* (Chicago: University of Chicago Press, 1979), 217a.

[2] William Barclay, *The Gospel of John, vol. 1* (Philadelphia: Westminster Press, 1956), 227-228.

[3] "Why Early Christians Were Despised," Christianity.com (accessed 05/20/2019).

[4] "Transubstantiation: A Fundamental Catholic Doctrine about the Eucharist," CatholicHOTDIST.com (accessed 05/20/2019).

[5] "Consubstantiation," Theopedia (accessed 05/21/2019).

[6] "Transubstantiation, Consubstantiation, or Something Else? Roman Catholic vs Protestant Views of The Lord's Supper," (Zondervan Academic, dtd 10/20/17) (accessed 05/21/2019).

[7] Reinhold Seeberg, *Text-Book of the History of Doctrines, pt. 2* (Grand Rapids: Baker Book House, 1954), 320-322.

[8] Lewis M. Hopfe and Mark R. Woodward, ed., *Religions of the World, 9th ed.* (Upper Saddle River, NJ: Pearson-Prentice Hall, 2005), 226.

[9] "The Basics of the Jewish Funeral," Chabad.org (accessed 06/13/2019).

[10] Rabbi Aryeh Kaplan, "The Soul," AISll.com (accessed 06/13/2019).

[11] William Barclay, "*The Gospel of John, vol. 2* (Philadelphia: Westminster Press, 1956), 115-116.

[12] Ibid., 119.

[13] Wilbert F. Howard, "The Gospel According to St. John, Exegesis," *The Interpreter's Bible, vol. 8* (New York: Abingdon Press, 1952), 648.

[14] Howard, *John*, 649.

[15] S. MacLean Gilmour, "The Gospel According to St. Luke, Exegesis," *The Interpreter's Bible, vol. 8* (New York: Abingdon Press, 1952), 70.

Nearing the End
(John 12:1-50)

PASSOVER/UNLEAVENED BREAD FESTIVAL
(12:1)

Passion Week is an established period at the end of the Incarnation story. Not all gospel records agree about the events and time sequences, but all agree that it occurs during the time of the Passover. Some background information/history about Passover can help with the dating and relationship of events:

- The one-day festival celebrates the deliverance and departure of the Hebrews from Egypt.
- The name and meaning come from the death plague "Passover" of Hebrew homes in the Exodus event (Exod. 12:1-14).
- Moses established the meal as roast lamb with unleavened bread and bitter herbs (Exod. 12:8).
- Moses instructed the Hebrews to remove all leaven before the Passover, leading to a ritual practice by faithful Jews to precede Passover with a diligent search of their home to ensure no leaven is present (Exod. 12:15).
- The Hebrews' departure was so abrupt, they had no time to prepare provisions, so they brought unleavened dough. Eating unleavened bread on their way out of Egypt in the Exodus became the basis for a seven-day Feast of Unleavened Bread, beginning at sundown on 15 Abib/Nisan (Exod. 12:39).
- The observance begins at sundown on the fourteenth day of the first Hebrew month (*Abib* —Canaanite name, Exod. 13:4/*Nisan*—Babylonian name, Neh. 2:1) and ends at sundown on 15 Abib/Nisan.

...

There is no indication in the Exodus 12 records that eating leaven in bread has a corrupt or evil factor in it. Other sources, however, write that in ancient Jewish literature leaven is a metaphor for evil, representing its corrupting effect as it ferments and permeates the entire dough as it causes the dough to rise.[1]

...

THE ANOINTING STORY
(12:2-11)

A week before the beginning of Passover, Jesus comes from Ephraim to Bethany, to the town of his friends, Mary, Martha, and Lazarus. They have supper; Martha serves; and Mary anoints the feet of Jesus. Lazarus is with them at the table, and a crowd gathers to see Lazarus and Jesus (vv. 2, 9).

Mary anoints the feet of Jesus with "costly ointment." It stirs questioning and criticism of the "waste" of the ointment instead of it being given to the poor. Jesus defends Mary on the basis that her act is an anointing in advance of his approaching burial. He tells those gathered, by contrast, that they will go on having opportunities to assist the poor.

A summary statement records the interest (curiosity?) of the crowd in Lazarus as one who has been raised from death. The living Lazarus is a problem for the Jewish leaders because his presence is an awe-inspiring witness to the people about Jesus. It is, in turn, leading to an increase in the number who believe in Jesus. The religious leaders plan, therefore, to kill Lazarus also to eliminate him as a problem.

For parallel study, Matthew 26:6-13 and Mark 14:3-9 record that this supper is held in the house of Simon the leper instead of the Lazarus family. Mary is not named as the anointer. Jesus' head is anointed instead of his feet. Judas is not identified as the complainer. Luke does not include this anointing in Bethany. Instead, in 7:36-50, Luke writes of an anointing in the house of Simon a Pharisee, with no place recorded and with significantly different details and teaching.

The references here to Lazarus being at the supper are the only records about the risen Lazarus. There is no recorded tradition about his risen life or his later death.

…

When Jesus reminds the people present that they will always have the poor, he states an ever-present truth: Poor who need help are always present. Human needs and opportunities for helpfulness in many forms are always at hand. Compassionate caring is a true Christian virtue, and Jesus is our most authentic example.

…

JESUS COMES TO JERUSALEM
(12:12-19)

John continues in chapter 12 with an account of the arrival of Jesus in Jerusalem and the beginning of what we describe as Holy Week. The Synoptic Gospels have more detailed versions, including the "cleansing" of the Temple. The generally accepted dating is that the entry into Jerusalem occurs on a Sunday (Palm Sunday), so the arrival at Bethany comes on a Sabbath (Saturday). The supper described in verses 1-11, which the Synoptics do not record, would have been in the evening after the end of the Sabbath (6:00 p.m.).

The entry of Jesus into the city is widely believed to be a messianic demonstration by him. The actions of the people, who make a celebratory event of his coming, indicate that the crowd understands it that way. Jesus rides into the city on a donkey. The people who witnessed the raising of Lazarus, and those who have heard about it from them, believe this wonder-working miracle by Jesus is a sign about him, so with zeal they are welcoming him in the hope that he is indeed their Messiah.

The Pharisees express among themselves their concern that they are losing their influence with the crowds.

The events of Holy Week convince me that there is a problem with understanding the entry into Jerusalem as a messianic demonstration. The statement that Jesus' ride on a donkey is a fulfillment of Zechariah 9:9 is an interpretation of that passage by the writers of Matthew and John. That passage in its historical setting is an oracle about conflict between Judah and adversary nations, and God's promise of victory for them. When the entry is believed to be messianic in fulfillment of Zechariah, it fits the traditional hope for the Messiah to be a God-anointed king who would vanquish oppressing adversaries and raise the Jewish nation as God's chosen people to exalted world dominance.

There is also in post-exilic Judaism a different messianic hope, one in which the Messiah will establish a universal kingdom of peace. Nonviolent harmony will prevail in nature, war will no longer occur in nations' relationships, and regathered/restored Israel will flourish (see Isaiah 11 and 61).

If Jesus intends the entry to be messianic, it is his declaration that he identifies with the hope for a kingdom of peace, and not a hope dependent on catastrophic violence. Ancient kings rode horses when leading their armies into battle. Riding a donkey is believed to be a sign that a person is coming in peace. Traditional understanding of this event is that Jesus comes riding on a donkey as a sign that he has come as Prince of Peace. Just as he has always presented himself, Jesus guards against and discourages any hint that any supernatural acts of ministry he does might lead to messianic demonstrations.

As the crowds who hail Jesus as a leader grow larger, the Jewish authorities sense that their positions of leadership, influence, and privilege are becoming more threatened, so their determination to eliminate him becomes stronger. This reaction shows clearly that they understand Jesus to be a "not to be dismissed" threat to them.

...

The events of Passion Week are about power and influence—who has it and what is its purpose? The history of Jewish religious leadership reveals that those leaders (and the people over whom they have influence) believe the purpose of their authority and power is to control the lives and actions of the people to keep them obedient to God. By the time Jesus lives, the Jewish leaders have come to believe that they alone know the truth about religion; that they are vested by God with authority to practice and enforce the requirements of their religion, and that their authority establishes them in positions of privilege and power.

Throughout his life and ministry, Jesus reveals an opposite meaning for the purposes of action and influence. When his disciples dispute among themselves about who is "greatest," Jesus says, "The kings of the Gentiles (those who are not God's people) 'lord it over them' (NIV) . . . but not so with you." By contrast he says to them, "I am among you as one who serves" (Luke 22:22-27). He tells them he has not come to "be served" but "to serve" (Mark 10:45). In the wilderness at the beginning of his ministry he "declines" to join demonic forces to gain control over people and "get glory" for himself (Matt. 4:8-10).

The actions by Jesus during the week leading up to his death on Friday reveal that he has come to the city to challenge the very meaning and purpose of power. He challenges both Jewish and Roman "powers" in Jerusalem, reveals their corrupt understanding of the meaning and purpose of power and influence, and defeats the effect of their "lord it over them" exercise of corrupt power. They prove they can kill him, but they cannot defeat and destroy him. They can only crucify his physical body. He triumphs over physical death. He lives. The powers of greed, ambition, self-centeredness, and evil are vanquished.

...

AMONG THE GATHERING PASSOVER CROWD
(12:20-36a)

Among the crowd coming to Jerusalem for the Passover festival are some Greeks. They approach the disciples about seeing Jesus. Andrew and Philip tell Jesus the Greeks are seeking him. Instead, Jesus begins talking about the significance of all that is happening.

The time is crucial. The Son of Man will be glorified. Jesus describes how it is necessary for a grain of wheat to be planted and give up its life-germ to produce fruit, but he does not relate this statement to his approaching death. He says again that loving your (physical) life more than your (spiritual) life can surely lead to loss in the latter (see Matt. 10:39, Mark 8:35, Luke 9:24). Jesus declares again that following him is essential to serving him and receiving favor from God (see Matt. 7:21, Luke 6:46).

Jesus then speaks about his own inner distress, but he declares he will not turn aside from this ominous time and situation. He uses the word "glorify" to describe what he is saying will happen shortly (see the commentary section below). He hears a voice affirming what he is doing. The crowd is divided about whether he hears an angel or they hear thunder.

Jesus makes a defining statement about what the events of that crucial time will mean in the "judgment of this world," and what will result from his being "lifted up" (see the commentary section below). Note that verse 33 is an interpretation by the writer of this gospel, not words from Jesus.

There is confusion among the crowd about what Jesus is saying. He does not answer with explanation, but rather gives them wise guidance about recognizing light (truth), paying heed to it, and walking (living) in it, to avoid living in "darkness" and suffering the consequences of it.

Both William Barclay and Arthur John Gossip describe Greeks as inquisitive, always searching, people who love "something-new."[2] Paul says the same about them (Acts 17:21). The Greeks in this passage, however, are interested in the religion of Judaism, for they are described as having come to worship. They are not described as proselytes, so likely they are God-fearers, or Gentiles who have become acquainted with Judaism and are sufficiently impressed by what they have learned about it to become "seekers."

While there for the Jewish festival they have heard enough about Jesus to be interested in learning more about him, maybe from him personally. The record does not indicate whether Jesus ever has any contact with the Greeks. Instead the record is about what Jesus teaches in response.

Jesus responds that the time has come and the Son of Man will be glorified. To many of the people steeped in Judaism, they hear this as a reference to the appearing of the Messiah and the beginning of his triumphal reign in an exalted Jewish nation. Jesus talks about a grain of wheat dying in order to produce new life. Such a statement calls to mind for them the "Suffering Servant" passages in Isaiah, especially in Isaiah chapter 53.

The difference between the two messianic traditions is confusing to many Jews. Throughout his ministry Jesus has taken the role of servant rather than reigning monarch. In the climactic end to his ministry through his approaching death he will give graphic meaning to the suffering role of ministry.

...

Note the references in this lengthy passage about the "Son of man being glorified" (v. 23), a "grain of wheat dying" (v. 24), "when I am lifted up from the earth" (v. 32), and "the Son of man must be lifted up" (v. 34). These statements have been traditionally understood as part of the nearly universal belief that the death of Jesus was a ritual blood sacrifice to "atone" for the sins of humankind.

Following are some things I have learned that Jesus says, or does not say, as they are recorded in the Gospels:

- *Jesus turns ideas about power, authority, greatness, and service upside down in relation to the ways they have been, and are, understood and practiced by people.*
- *Jesus describes his rejection, execution, and death to be a result of Jewish religious leaders' belief that his "religion is blasphemy" and his "crowd popularity" is a threat to their leadership positions among the Jews, and their responsibility to maintain order for the occupying Romans.*
- *Jesus self-identifies with the stream of messianic hope that focuses on a "kingdom" of harmony with God and "caring peace" among people.*
- *Jesus does not describe his death as a substitutionary blood sacrifice in atonement for human guilt resulting from original sin.*
- *Jesus does not "foretell" that his death will be by crucifixion.*
- *Jesus uses forms of the word "glorify" to refer to events of the Passion only in the Gospel of John.*

I readily identify as one who believes the Gospel of John is a theologically oriented account of the life and teachings of Jesus. It seems obvious that the writer feels free to alter, expand, and compose sections based on two guidelines. The focal use of "signs" to describe things said and done as revealing the divine nature and purpose of incarnation is both central and unique. The writer states this purpose of his approach in John 20:20-21, "These [signs] . . . are written that you may believe that Jesus is the Christ, the Son of God, and that believing you may have life in his name."

The crowd described in this passage is confused by any talk about Jesus dying. His entry into the city is believed by the crowd to be a messianic event. A part of the varied beliefs among the Jews about their hoped-for messiah is that he would not be subject to death. "Messiah" and "death" are contradictory opposites to them.

In the Fourth Gospel the words "glorify" and "lifted up" are both used in unique ways. They have come to have specific (and questionable) meanings in traditional Christian tenets of faith. Lifted up (John 3:14, 8:28, 12:32, 12:34) is widely understood to mean crucified. As I write above about John 3:14, the "lifting up" of the serpent in the wilderness (Num. 21:4-9) is the "lifting up" of an object of faith for Israelites to trust and receive healing. The bronze serpent is not lifted up as a sacrifice. The purpose of "lifting up" the Son of Man is for "whoever" to "believe in him." The concept of "lifting up" can readily mean "holding forth" that people may know about, evaluate, and choose whether to believe in, trust, and follow. The same idea is present in epiphany (manifestation in 2 Tim. 1:10).[3]

Glorified (John 7:39, 12:16, 12:23, 12:28, 13:31-32) is also widely understood to refer to the death of Jesus. Glory, by definition and by use throughout the Bible, means renown, magnificence, supremacy. Glorify is a verb that means to bestow glory on, to proclaim the glory of, to praise the glory of. Obviously, we cannot bestow glory on God: in his infinite deity everything that glory means, God already has in perfection. We can proclaim the glory of God to others, and we can praise the glory of God in worship. But how will the glory of the Son and the Father be shown forth by death? William Barclay writes about this passage that "by glorified He (Jesus) meant crucified," and he writes further that Jesus "was saying that only by death comes life."[4]

John's emphasis on "signs" that reveal who Jesus is and what he is about throws light on the meaning of "glorify" in this gospel. His coming crucifixion will not be a "sign" of God's "glory" to his followers. Their hopeless despondency as they entomb his body and prepare to embalm the body after the Sabbath will reveal a sense of utter defeat. But Paul writes that he is shown to be . . . the Son of God . . . "by his resurrection from the dead" (Rom. 1:4). The victory of life over death is the glorifying "sign" Jesus promises as he prays, "Father, glorify your name . . . (show forth your glory as the giver of life)."

Jesus will be "glorified" (his awesome majesty revealed) when he "presents himself alive after his passion" (Acts 1:3). Jesus is lifted up when he is made known by "visible manifestation" (incarnation). Jesus is glorified when his "hidden divinity" is revealed and he is shown forth as worthy of trust, praise, and commitment. His renown and supreme grace continue to be shown forth when he is "lifted up" in the lives and witness of people who trust him and live out his grace, forgiveness, and help in transformed lives.

. . .

In verses 35-36, Jesus turns the focus of the interchange away from messianic matters to encourage the crowd to pay attention to the difference between light and darkness, between truth and untruth, between the passing and the lasting.

These concluding words by Jesus reflect a truth he has tried to reveal all through his ministry. He tries repeatedly to help people unlearn what they have come to believe about the role of their hoped-for messiah, namely, that he has not come to be a nationalistic military leader and reigning monarch. Jesus has come to bring light into the world, the light of truth that God is a loving, outreaching, forgiving, gracious God whose yearning heart is focused on bringing sinful people of all the world and of all ages into a reconciled harmony of fellowship with himself. In his preaching Jesus declares that such reconciling harmony can come to be real only as sinners believe in the gospel (the good news that God is that kind of God), as they believe that truth enough to trust God, and in trusting God they repent (change their minds about what is valuable and lasting in life enough to change the values by which they live). Jesus teaches that this trusting, repenting, and becoming reconciled will be such a dynamic and transforming experience that it will result in a person being "born again," i.e. by the grace of God having a new beginning in life, leading to a new life in which the spiritual is more important than the physical, in which one's relationship with God is more to be valued than anything that can be gained from the temporary values of this physical life. This is what Jesus means by "becoming sons of light."

UNBELIEF . . . WHY?
(12:36b-43)

Jesus ends the interchange that began by the request of God-fearing Greeks (Gentiles) to see Jesus. He leaves the crowd and goes away alone. The writer summarizes that though the crowd has seen the "signs," they still have not come to believe in what Jesus is teaching, doing, and revealing.

The writer interprets the situation to have a fated element in it. He describes his hearers' lack of belief as a fulfillment of a prophecy by Isaiah that their inability to believe is caused by God to make them unable to see truth and believe it. In spite of this "blinding" by God, many people—even some of the Levites and scribes—do believe in Jesus, but for fear of the Pharisees they do not dare confess their faith in Jesus openly. The Pharisees have opposed Jesus so firmly that they have ordered anyone who declares faith in Jesus to be expelled from the Jewish synagogues. John concludes with a scathing condemnation, effectively calling them cowards who love popularity more than being right with God.

. . .

The quotations from the Old Testament book of Isaiah should be understood as a witness about Isaiah's concern for the hardness of heart and disbelief in his own generation (Isa. 6:9), not as an inspired prophecy of what is described about the crowd's response to Jesus. This reference used here describes Jewish belief in the eighth century BC. This is not what Jesus taught and practiced. I do not find Jesus ever teaching or asking anything of his hearers that they are not fully able to choose and do. Jesus always deals with people as though they are gifted with freedom of choice and capacity of will, making us fully able to choose what to believe or disbelieve; to choose which values to live by and which to not embrace, and having made a choice to be able by set of will to follow a chosen course in life. Jesus never hinted, however, that we are left on our own to pursue our way through life. There are precious promises about God's gracious presence in the Holy Spirit to give light and inspiration, to help us choose and live out our choices if they are good ones.

...

AWESOME MEANINGFUL WORDS
(12:44-50)

The last few verses of John 12 cover the conclusion of Jesus' public teaching ministry. Jesus declares a total unity between himself and the Father, both in what he is revealing and in how people are responding. He states the purpose of his incarnate presence is to bring light to provide truth for people to believe and follow. His sayings are not about judgment and condemnation, for his mission is about salvation. Whoever rejects his sayings "has a judge" in the present and will be judged "on the last day" by response to his "words spoken." His last public declaration is that he will not be separated from the Father by anything he says and does.

...

In John 3:17-18 and again in John 12:46-48 a significant truth about incarnation is set forth. God's purpose in incarnation is not judgment, condemnation, and punishment. Sinful persons are "walking in darkness" and "perishing" in alienation from harmony with God. Both aBaD (Hebrew) and apoletai (Greek), which are translated "perish," mean "to lose life and be destroyed by lack of sustenance or security" (see Ps. 1:6; Matt. 8:25; Luke 8:24, 15:17; John 3:15, 10:28). To perish results from being deprived, not from being punished.

Jesus reveals that God is not so offended by sinfulness that he requires fitting punishment to establish justice before forgiveness and grace can be bestowed. Jesus reveals by incarnate life and teaching that God is so loving and compassionate that he is forever outreaching, offering forgiveness and reconciliation for all who will respond in repentant faith, trust, and commitment of life. In these concluding verses of his public teaching, Jesus says that those who will not trust what he teaches will be judged by their rejection of him and the truths he reveals.

...

NOTES

¹J. Edgar Park, "The Book of Exodus, Exposition," *The Interpreter's Bible, vol. 1* (New York: Abingdon Press, 1952), 920b.

²William Barclay, *The Gospel of John, vol. 2,* (Philadelphia: Westminster Press, 1956), 139-40. Arthur John Gossip, "The Gospel of St. John, Exposition," *The Interprteter's Bible, vol. 8* (New York: Abingdon Press, 1952), 661.

³William F. Arndt and F. Wilbur Gingrich, *Walter Bauer's Greek-English Lexicon of the New Testament," 2ⁿᵈ ed.* (Chicago: University of Chicago Press, 1979), 304a.

⁴Barclay, *John,* 143.

The Last Evening
(John 13:1–17:26)

John devotes seven chapters to the last twenty-four hours of Jesus' physical life. Chapters 13:1–17:26 tell of the evening spent with the disciples in an upper room. Chapters 18:1–19:16 give an account of the arrest and trial of Jesus. Chapter 19:17-42 tells of the crucifixion and entombment. Except for the exposure and departure of Judas (13:21-30) and the warning that Peter would deny Jesus (13:36-38), there are no parallels in the Synoptics about the hours spent with the other eleven disciples.

The volume of teaching included, and the almost uninterrupted nature of the presentation, lead many interpreters to describe this as a composed record gathered from earlier teaching by Jesus. The sequence of subjects leads some interpreters to attempt to reorder the teachings. In this volume we will follow the text as we have it in our familiar Bibles. The four chapters (13–16) of last evening teaching include some of the most significant of all the teachings of Jesus. John writes them as the last evening upper room discourse by Jesus for his disciples.

GATHERING FOR A LAST SUPPER
(13:1)

The events of the evening take place before the beginning of Passover. Jesus knows the timing and crucial nature of the evening. He plans the evening, motivated by his love for his disciples, his awareness of imminent death, and his desire for one last evening with them. As he says later in the evening, he still has many things to say to them (16:12).

Different sources set differing times for the events of the night. The following sequence is best supported by the recorded data:

1. The Last Supper takes place after sundown on Thursday.
2. Late Thursday evening, Jesus and his disciples go from the upper room to the Garden of Gethsemane.
3. Judas leads the officers to Gethsemane to arrest Jesus.
4. Jesus is kept under Jewish control through the remainder of Thursday night and through the Jewish trials in the early dawn of Friday.

5. Jesus is taken before Pilate for the Roman trial, conviction, and execution.
6. Crucifixion takes place about midmorning on Friday.
7. Jesus dies by midafternoon and is entombed before sundown, the beginning of Passover Sabbath.

AN EXAMPLE ABOUT HUMILITY
(13:2-17)

Judas Iscariot is present with the Jesus and the other disciples, although he is already set in his intention to betray Jesus to the Jewish authorities. He does not leave until later, however (v. 30).

Jesus does an incredibly characteristic but surprisingly unexpected thing. He takes the role of servant and washes the disciples' feet. Simon Peter objects. Jesus explains, "This is not about cleansing, but about belonging."

Conversation around the table follows. Jesus talks with the disciples about the significance of the foot washing. They have come to recognize and accept his role among them as Teacher and Lord. So, he tells them, his action shall be an example to them, that they should be the kind of people and follow the attitude and practices he has exemplified among them.

Jesus continues to teach them a lesson about status and conduct. The greater is superior to the subordinate, the Creator greater than the creature, the master greater that the servant, the teacher greater than the student. Status and character are not the same. Character determines the way we live out the status role we have. Jesus has revealed that greatness is not determined by status, but by the quality of conduct (v. 17).

The Synoptic Gospels record details about the Last Supper that are the basis for the almost universal Christian practice of the Lord's Supper (Eucharist). John only records that they share a meal. The record of foot-washing, by 'contrast, is unique to John.

The disciples are familiar with this common practice. It is customary in their culture for a host to have a servant wash the feet of guests who come into his house. The roads are unpaved and people walk in primitive footwear, so guests' feet are either muddy or dusty. To have their feet washed is refreshing and is considered an honor. The task is usually assigned to a slave or a hired servant, and the washing is usually done upon arrival as part of the welcoming rituals.

Neither Jesus nor his disciples have slaves or hired servants. No one is assigned to that task as they gather. Jesus has often taught that service to another is an expression of kindness and regard for the person being served. He chooses to be a servant, to show kindness and love for his disciples, and to teach them a lesson that will live with them and inspire us. His action astounds his disciples. Simon Peter reacts, as he does so often, with an immediate response. Jesus, in turn, explains that his action is figurative: it demonstrates the value of the relationship between them and the value of having a serving spirit.

The Fourth Gospel indicates that Judas, the betrayer, is present for both the dinner and the foot-washing. Then, after exposure, he leaves. Luke also writes that Judas leaves after the sharing of bread and cup (22:17-22).

...

William Barclay has a splendid discussion about the presence of Judas at the supper and the foot-washing. He contrasts the depth of both treachery and hypocrisy on the part of Judas to be there, with the "last appeal of love" on the part of Jesus to allow him to still be present. Barclay concludes, "It is always night when a man turns his back on Jesus Christ."[1]

...

JESUS AND JUDAS
(13:18-30)

Jesus becomes very personal, manifesting his troubled spirit as he begins to share with the group that a betrayer is among them. He describes what is happening as like the treachery of "my bosom friend in whom I trusted, who ate my bread, (and) has lifted his heel against me" (Ps. 41:9).

The disciple group is taken aback and confused about who that could be. Judas has been so carefully deceptive in hiding his treacherous soul and his treasonous plan that his fellow disciples do not even suspect him. He cannot fool Jesus, who knows what is in his heart. Jesus exposes Judas by handing him a piece of bread from the table, but the disciples still do not comprehend what he is doing. Judas goes out, and it is night.

...

Day and night, light and darkness, life and death, the world and the Kingdom: All are contrasts used to teach lessons about choices people make, differing values by which people live, and fateful consequences that result from those choices and values. In the Gospels two ways are set forth:

1. *Responding in repentant faith and trust in the gospel revelation that God loves, seeks to reconcile, and freely forgives sinfulness*
2. *Loving darkness, denying or ignoring the gospel revelation, and living in alienation from God*

The affirmations in the Gospels teach that repentant faith and new birth reconcile with God and enhance life with the blessings of grace (eternal life, abundant life). Alienation from God, on the other hand, causes a person to perish (John 3:16). The meaning of "perishing" needs to be clearly understood. Perishing is a condition resulting from being deprived of sustaining nurture. It is not a punitive concept, resulting from guilt of evil. Spiritual depravity results from wrong choices and neglect of spiritual nurture. Perishing is slow, often unaware, but insidious and certain, and with lasting even to eternal consequences. Judas chose "the night."

...

A NEW COMMANDMENT FOR HIS FOLLOWERS
(13:31-35)

After the departure of Judas, Jesus says to the remaining disciples, "Now is the Son of man glorified." He follows by saying that he will shortly be gone from them and they will not be able to come where he is going. To prepare the disciples for living through the trauma of his absence, and for their life ahead as disciples and witnesses, Jesus gives them a "new" commandment: "Love one another; even as I have loved you."

Use of the term "glorified" following the departure of Judas raises again an understanding of its meaning (see discussion of John 12:20-36a). Here, as above, the traditional interpretation is that glorify refers to Jesus' death. John's emphasis on signs seems to mean that Jesus' victory of life over death is the clearer manifestation of the glory of God. In John 14:13, 15:8, and 17:4—all records from the last evening—the term glorify is used to mean ways that God's glory is revealed, with none of them in relation to the death of Jesus (note the span of glory reflected in John 17:1-5).

It is important to understand what Jesus means by the glory of God if we are to understand what Jesus means by loving one another as he has loved us. There is a long tradition behind the Second Great Commandment to love your neighbor "as yourself" (Lev. 19:18, Matt. 22:39). Jesus raises the standard for those who would be his disciples: they will love each other "as I have loved you."

...

The earliest human ideas about deities (God, gods) was about the greatness of divine power as creator and controller of the material universe. The "power of God/god" emphasis prevailed among primitive people in ancient polytheistic nature religions. After the Israelites had a king who built for himself a royal court and reigned in palatial majesty (1 Kgs. 4:21-28), there developed a concept among them that God is like the king—only raised to greater levels of splendor, "enthroned in the heavens"

(Ps. 103:19), surrounded by a majestic court (Ps. 93:1, 20:6). Power and majestic splendor become the prevailing images of glory (See Rev. 4:2-6).

Jesus does not portray an image of God as a reigning monarch centered in a majestic heavenly court. His only prominent references to "holy angels" are in end-time descriptions (Matt. 16:27 with parallels in Mark 8:38 and Luke 9:26; Matt. 24:31 with parallels in Mark 13:27; and Matt. 25:31). The more prominent image of God portrayed by Jesus is of a Loving Father at one in incarnate revelation and ministry with the Son.

When Jesus talks about love, he refers to the agape *quality of caring that is outwardly focused and unselfishly centered on the persons in his care. He describes the true meaning of greatness as service to make the world better and to enhance the lives of others. That is the standard to which he calls his disciples if they are to love one another as he has loved them (loves us). God is glorified when the truly majestic greatness of his goodness is made manifest in our lives who are identified as disciples of Jesus.*

...

JESUS AND SIMON PETER
(13:36-38)

Simon Peter questions Jesus about where he is going that they cannot follow. He then brashly vows that he will lay down his life for Jesus. Jesus does not explain to the disciples what will happen in his death, but he does warn Simon that before dawn he will deny Jesus.

Referring to his imminent death, Jesus says that he will shortly be gone from among them and they cannot come with him (v. 33), as they have been going about with him since they became his disciples. Traumatic change is about to come upon the disciples.

Simon Peter, as he often does, speaks up with a question, "Where are you going, and why can't I go with you?" Jesus replies by casting his statement in terms of present and future. His death will be in the present, and their deaths will be in the future. But Peter is not satisfied with that answer. He declares that he is ready to follow Jesus now, and will die with him if that is necessary. Jesus is gentle but frank with Peter. He asks, "Will you lay down your life for me?" as much as to ask, "Do you really know what you are saying? Do you even begin to realize the meaning of what is about to happen?" Jesus warns Peter that the peril of that very night will cause him to default on his declaration of loyalty and deny him.

A COMFORTING PROMISE
(14:1-7)

Jesus turns in his conversation with the disciples to give them hopeful promises that will help to sustain them through the peril, turmoil, and fear that will break upon them before the night ends and through the coming days. With deep caring concern for his disciples in the face of his imminent death, Jesus encourages them to believe in God and in him. They will see him die, they will believe that hope has been crushed, and they will fear for their own lives.

Jesus assures them that he will still care about them, preparing for a time when they will "follow him where he is going," as he promised (13:37). They are confused and ask for an explanation. Jesus then speaks a momentous truth about himself (v. 6), about his unity with the Father, and about the disciples' relationship with him and the Father beyond the trauma that is about to sweep over them.

When life is filled with distress, when danger (real or imagined) strikes fear into you, nothing can give assurance and a sense of security more than trust in God. Jesus speaks to the disciples about the certainty of God's prevailing presence and sovereignty. God's "house" is established, and there are "abiding places" in preparation for them.

A brief word about words describing our "place" with God: The Greek word in the text about "mansions" or "rooms" has a basic meaning of "places of abiding," or "dwelling places," or "a place where you can be at home." The familiar and well-loved words "many mansions" are not specific to the text but were used by the translators of the KJV to represent the majesty that belongs to the glorious presence of God.

The next phrase, "if it were not so," refers back to Jesus' assurance and promise that in the Father's care there is security in times of peril and ultimately after death. The phrase is followed in some translations with a declaration, "I would have told you." Other translations follow the phrase with a question, "Would I have told you?" Both translations have Jesus promise "assurance" of certain provision by God. The Greek *ei de me* ("but" "if" "not," or "otherwise") supports the more positive declaration.

Jesus relates the meaning of his imminent death to the assurance of his promise: his "going" and "preparing" will have inherent within them a "making ready" for them to come after him. He had promised the disciples (13:36) that they could follow him later, that "where I am you may be also (14:3).

His statement that they know "where" and "the way" leaves them confused. Thomas voices their confusion, and his question leads to an answer by Jesus, which is one of the most familiar and often quoted passages from the entire Bible: "I am the way, the truth, and the life." Jesus further declares that knowing him is the same as knowing the Father.

...

Knowing Jesus and the Father is the way to knowing truth, knowing the truth that is in them is the way to life—the way, the truth, and the life. That is as basic a truth as has ever broken upon the minds and hearts of humankind. To know Jesus and follow him in faith is the way to transformation of life, new birth of spirit, and reconciliation with God. This "I AM" saying is indeed a declaration by Jesus about the meaning, purpose, and result of his incarnate coming.

...

UNCERTAINTY SEEKS AN ANSWER
(14:8-11)

Philip makes a request of Jesus: "Lord, show us the Father." Jesus replies that through their time together he has revealed the Father, and again affirms the unity between himself and the Father. He urges them to pay careful attention to what he has been doing, as much as to say, "I have been doing 'God-kind-of-things' among you."

Philip's request reflects what has been an ages-long human problem: our inability to discern what spiritual life without physical form is like. That inability has been behind practices since ancient times.

The Old Testament records that polytheistic people planted trees, set up stone pillars, and carved idols because they wanted to attract a "god" to come dwell (to embody themselves in a material entity) and be pleased to bring fruitful blessings. It was the basis of the practice in Baal nature worship. It was also behind the actions of some disobedient Hebrews, who in violation of the command to make no graven images of their God, nevertheless, crafted material items to worship. The same difficulty is reflected in the long-practiced descriptions of God as having human physical features (eyes, hand, feet, voice, etc.). It is still reflected in the concepts that are common in end-time descriptions of heaven as found in the figurative visions in the Book of Revelation.

The confusion among the disciples reveals that, in spite of their time spent personally with Jesus, they sometimes do not discern the "signs" emphasized in this gospel any more clearly than people in the crowds. In these verses Jesus describes the unity between himself and the Father in relation to his incarnate mission among humanity. Since human persons have such difficulty understanding the nature and character of God who is Spirit (see John 4:24), God chose to become incarnate as God the Son, living as a fully human person to reveal for us the nature and character of God. Mankind had not before been able to grasp the reality of God as eternal spirit.

Note this statement in verse 9: "He who has seen me has seen the Father." Jesus continues to explain that his words and works are one and the same as the Father. He encourages them, that if they cannot grasp what that unity means by his words, to take note of his works. What he has been doing is the same as a God whose character of caring love, compassionate kindness, and reconciling forgiveness will surely do.

THOSE WHO BELIEVE WILL FOLLOW
(14:12)

Having described the unity that belongs to God, Father and Son, Jesus speaks to the disciples of the unity that should (shall) belong to the relationship between himself and his followers. Believing in Jesus will lead to "doing the same works," or living the same kind of lives. Jesus even says that those "who believe in me" will do greater works. He says this will happen "because" I go the the Father.

"Believing in me" and doing the "works that I do" are affirmations underlying the entire gospel. Jesus teaches that "believing in me" means "trusting in who I am and what I am revealing." He reveals that this "believing/trusting" response is the basis for a repentant faith relationship between a believer and himself.

A repentant faith response, in turn, results in a new birth beginning of a transformed life in harmony with God.

This new spiritual life is the basis on which Jesus says a person who "believes" in him "will do" the same kind of works.

Doing "greater works" seems surely to describe more in number, not greater in nature. While he is physically incarnate, Jesus accepts the physical limitations of time and place. The disciples are more in number and will be physically present and active in ministry in more places and among more people. Jesus relates this expansion of ministry by the disciples to his "going" to the Father. During the last evening Jesus is seeking to help the disciples begin to be prepared for the time after he is no longer physically with them. All of the last evening discourse is set within the context of his imminent death. His promises about the Paraclete that follow immediately are central to the preparation he is doing.

THE HELP (HELPER) YOU WILL HAVE
(14:13-26)

Jesus will be executed the next day. The disciples will be cast down into despair. What will Jesus' words about "doing greater works" mean at sundown tomorrow?

Jesus says forthrightly that he will not "leave them comfortless, desolate." The Greek is more personal: "abandoned as orphans." He promises that both Father and Son will still be active in their lives, helping with answered prayers. Then Jesus makes an awesome promise: the Father will "give you another Paraclete" (v. 16). Jesus identifies the Paraclete as "the Spirit of truth" (v. 17) and "the Holy Spirit" (v. 26).

In his following discussion Jesus tells the disciples frankly that soon the "world will see me no more" (v. 19), but he will not be absent from them (vv. 19-20). The disciples do not understand. How can he "be manifest" to them and not to other people (the world)? Jesus promises that the Father and I "will make our home with him (you)" (v. 23). The Paraclete will also be an abiding presence who will "teach them" and bring "to their remembrance" all that Jesus has said (v. 26).

Jesus promises the relationship between himself and his disciples will not end with his physical death on Friday. The change from physical relationship to spiritual relationship is difficult for the disciples to grasp. Prayers offered to the Father and answers anticipated are not new for them. Jesus receiving and answering prayers will be new.

A vital feature of their ongoing relationship is reflected in the statement by Jesus, "If you love me, you will keep my commandments." This is *agape* language. Its distinctiveness is important. Although they are sometimes used interchangeable, *agape* and *phileo* are different in their focus. *Agape* means esteem and refers to the value with which I hold you, and the care I have for you. (You are important to me.) *Phileo* means how I feel about you. (Do I like you and find you pleasant to have around?) *Agape* is used consistently in the New Testament to refer to God's love for humanity.[2] Jesus says (paraphrased and amplified), "If you care about what I want life for you and all you touch to be like, if the values I have taught you are the things you believe are important enough to invest your life in, then you will strive to live as I have instructed you."

Jesus continues, "If we have this harmony of relationship, then this is what I will do." He promises to ask the Father and assures them that the Father will give them another Paraclete (variously translated Comforter, Counselor, Advocate).

. . .

The promise of a Paraclete is a revealing promise. This word that Jesus uses is a compound word in Greek. Para is a preposition meaning "alongside." Kaleo is a verb meaning "to call, to summon." Paraclete (Parakleton) means "one called alongside." Jesus identifies the Paraclete clearly as "The Spirit of Truth, Holy Spirit."

Traditionally, the meaning of Paraclete has been understood to mean that the Holy Spirit is called alongside to help us when in our need we call on him in prayer. My deep conviction is that God wants so much to "lead us in paths of righteousness" and "pursue us with goodness and mercy" that he is "called (drawn) by his Agape *love" to always abide with us to guide and help. I understand Paraclete to mean that God cares so deeply for us that he cannot make himself leave us to our own hopeless course of sinful life.*

This passage in John 14 has more rich meaning. Jesus promises that the Father will give them "another Paraclete." The Greek language has two words meaning "another": eteros ("another of a different kind") and allos ("another of the same kind"). Jesus seems surely to be describing himself as a Paraclete who has been drawn by a loving heart that "called him" alongside the disciples in incarnation to do a redeeming, reconciling work among humankind. This new Paraclete will be the Holy Spirit who will abide with God's people forever, in contrast to Jesus who has been a Paraclete of the same kind, but present in "human form," whose presence will end shortly in his death.

Jesus describes the Holy Spirit as a Paraclete that the world cannot see or know, and therefore cannot lay hands on and snatch from them, as the Jewish authorities will that very night arrest Jesus and by scheming manipulation get him killed. The Holy Spirit will be a real Paraclete to them, another of the same kind as Jesus has been. They have come to experience and trust that Jesus is God with them. The Holy Spirit will come to be so real to them that they will sense the Spirit's presence as God with them. "He will be in you."

Jesus summarizes his Paraclete promises by a personal promise: "I will not leave you desolate; I will come to you." His words are graphic: "I will not leave you as orphans," abandoned without anyone to guide you, anyone for you to belong to. In the face of the imminent arrest and execution of Jesus, these are dynamic and positive assurances by Jesus to the disciples to help them through the fear and drama of the coming days. They continue as uplifting and inspiring promises for all people in all ages who trust in Jesus and the Holy Spirit as Emmanuel, God with us.

...

Jesus goes on to explain in more detail what is about to happen. Shortly, so far as the world is concerned, he will be "dead and gone," and will be seen no more. But just as he has promised the disciples that he will come to them, he assures them that they will see him again "in a little while." His living again, triumph over death, will assure them that they will live. Through it all, unity of the Son with the Father, and unity of the Father and the Son with the disciples, will become clearly established and made known.

Here, so very near the end of his incarnate life, Jesus gives personal meaning to his followers about the meaning of the relationship between them. To have his commandments and keep them will establish a relation based on love. The disciples do not understand what Jesus is promising.

Judas (not Iscariot, but Thaddeus—see Matt. 10:3) asks how the relationship will be different "with them" from "with the world." Jesus explains that the difference will be in the way they will respond in love, faith, and obedience and the way the "world" will not. This is *agape* talk.

Jesus is describing a relationship that is more than "we like each other." He is saying that we "care so much about each other" that each other's "well-being" will be as important as (or even more so) our concern for ourselves. He affirms again that what he has taught and promised them is what he has brought to them from the Father. To affirm further the unity between the Father, himself, and the Holy Spirit, Jesus assures them that the Holy Spirit will help them remember and understand the meaning of what he has said.

A PROMISE OF PEACE
(14:27-31)

Jesus gives consoling assurance to the disciples with a promise about peace. He promises a peace different than that of the world.

Jesus encourages them to hold steadfastly to the peace that faith and assurance affords so that they will be able to live through the imminent turmoil of the next days without troubled and fearful hearts. He reminds them that while he has talked with them about "going away," he has also told them that he is going "to the Father." This gives them cause to rejoice because the greatness of the Father will assure final overcoming and not defeat.

In summary comments Jesus tells the disciples to remember what he has told them ahead of coming events. He says he has done this in preparation to help them not lose faith and hope. He urges them to remember that he and the Father are at one in what he is doing.

John 17:1 reads like it should follow John 14:31. Two chapters of intervening teaching continue to record what surely seems to be more of the evening's upper room conversation by Jesus to his disciples.

...

What is the peace that the world gives? Too often "the world" means the world of evil people where violence, greed, and conflict cause hurt, fear, and distress. People, not just evil people, long for an absence of distress from the troubles that threaten their longed-for calm for the pursuit of life. But that is only a part of the "peace the world gives," and it may well be the smaller part for many of us.

One of the most tempting and deceitful dangers we meet in our daily lives is our tendency to overvalue the physical aspects of life and undervalue the spiritual dimensions of life. We have physical senses and live in a temporal and material environment. It is easy to drift into a way of life obsessed with the needs and pleasures of our physical lives. "Peace" can easily come to mean adequate time and resources to "enjoy" good health, pleasant activities, and "good times." The affluence that has enabled many people in contemporary life to become sports- and entertainment-obsessed is a reflection of this "peace that the world gives."

In the significant context of the evening before his death, Jesus tells his followers that this is not the kind of peace he gives. The vital difference seems to lie in the fact that the "peace the world gives" is about the temporariness of physical life. His great affirmation that "where your treasure is, there will your heart be also" (Matt. 6:21) stands as an ever-present warning from Jesus for us to be careful about the values and priorities we choose for our lives.

What, then, is the "peace that Jesus gives"? In the face of the certain unease, fear, and turmoil that will erupt on their lives with his crucifixion the next morning, Jesus says to the disciples, "My peace I leave with you." What they will have to sustain them through the days ahead will certainly not be about "what you shall eat," nor "what you shall drink," nor "what you shall wear." What will leave them afraid and hiding behind closed doors is whether they will die as Jesus has died.

What makes for peace when your life is on the line? Jesus has revealed by teaching and by living example that God is like a loving Father who can be trusted because his character is beneficent, and his heart yearns to hold us in harmony as "prodigal sons who were blind but who now see." Jesus has proclaimed in his preaching that the "kingdom of God is at hand"; that God is sovereign, here and now, everywhere and always.

As Eternal Sovereign, God establishes by his creative action both natural and moral laws in the very foundation of the physical universe and of human life. God determines how natural law works in material things. God has also established the values of life by which human life is enhanced or degraded.

Jesus taught a lot about faith and trust, about believing his teaching enough to follow him, and about trusting the God of grace to bring "abundant life" to reality in one's life. The peace that Jesus gives is largely about assurance, about confidence of reconciled harmony with God, about hope for "eternal life" to flourish after physical death. The peace that Jesus gives is a spiritual reality that sustains a person in life and in the face of death.

…

VINE AND BRANCHES
(15:1-11)

The final "I AM" saying is placed in chapter 15 by the writer of John as part of the final evening's teaching. By the dependence of branches on the vine for life and the ability to bear fruit, Jesus describes the vital importance of the relationship of the disciples to him and the Father. He says that their relationship with God is, and will be, the very source through which his followers will have their life and their fruitfulness. They have come to have faith in him through their life shared with him during his incarnate life among them. Now that he will be taken from them, he urges them to be steadfast in their faith and to "abide in him." The disciples are not vines; they are branches. They have a new life in spirit through their relationship of faith and trust in God, Father, and Son.

Applying the example of a vineyard, Jesus says that fruitful branches are pruned to help them become more fruitful. Branches that are not fruitful are removed from the vine to wither and die. Fruitful branches are fruitful only because they are abiding in the vine. Those who abide in the vine are those who believe "my words" and who keep "my commandments," who "love me" and abide in "my love" for them.

Jesus is preparing the disciples for the great change they will experience. He tells them he is going away, but assures them that they will not be abandoned. He promises that God will give "another Paraclete" to abide with them forever, who the world will not be able to take from them. But Jesus knows his death will leave them feeling like "branches stripped from their mother vine." Branches can only live "in the vine." Jesus wants them to not forget. Jesus instructs them to ask (pray), keep commandments, bear fruit, and abide in God's love. Fear will almost overcome. Hope will almost fail. Darkness will almost win. But "you will see me; because I live, you will live also" (14:19).

Jesus also assures the disciples that in their ongoing lives, as they bear fruit, the Father will "prune" them (an improving concept, not a correcting concept). Here Jesus seems to bring forward the "Paraclete" promise he has made earlier, that the Holy Spirit will "teach them 'all things' and bring to their remembrance the things he had told them" (14:26). The ongoing presence, guidance, and help of the Holy Spirit will provide their "pruning" and "enabling" to help them become more fruitful.

...

The truths Jesus set forth that evening in the vine and branches figure are essentially applicable to Christians in every age. Only in a living relationship of faith, trust, and commitment can anyone have an authentic "life hid with Christ in God" (see Col. 3:3). And only as we live as "branches abiding in the vine" can we be fruitful in fulfilling our prayer with Jesus that "God's kingdom come and God's will be done on earth as in heaven." In a summary sentence Jesus tells all his followers that faithful abiding and fruitful living will be the key to fulfilling and joy-filled lives.

...

LOVE AND FRIENDSHIP LIVED OUT
(15:12-17)

Jesus continues to talk about the importance of a communal relationship among his followers, characterized by "caring love" for each other. Earlier (13:34), he called it a new commandment when he urged them to love one another as he has loved them. Here he says that "no one" can have a "greater love [*agape*]" for anyone than to be willing to "lay down his life (soul)" for "a friend."

Jesus gives "friends" a special meaning. Not only does Jesus choose to have them around him as servants/disciples; he also chooses to share with them intimate truths they cannot know apart from his making them known. As friends, he is preparing them for a "fruitful" life, which means far more than just productive work. Jesus reminds them again about the vital importance of "caring love for each other" through the crisis of his death and for their lives ahead.

The statements about "greater love" and "laying down one's life" for a friend surely have special meaning for the disciples as they live through the following days (if they are able to remember them in the turmoil and trauma of those days). The statements have meaning that make them far more broadly applicable than the specific time and setting of that evening.

The words translated "lay down for" (*the/tithemi, huper*) are also used to mean "put upon/lay across/set the heart on, for/on behalf of."[3] This passage refers to Jesus dying for his friends. One of the reasons for his physical death is "on their behalf." The end of the Incarnation will be followed by the gift of the Holy Spirit (John 16:7). The word translated "life" is *psuchen* (breath of life, soul).[4] This allows for a more expansive understanding of these words of Jesus.

...

The concept of soul refers to the totality of the self, the person, physical body, and spiritual soul. To lay down one's life for a friend can surely mean to die physically to protect another from dying. To lay down one's life for (on behalf of) another can also mean investing one's life for the benefit of another. A mother can literally "lay down" (use up) her life caring for a disabled child. A teacher or physician can "lay down" (devote his/her life) for the education and medical care of his/her students and patients. The motivation, one's caring love for another, is what makes the difference.

Paul uses an expression that is appropriate here. He appeals, "present your bodies as a living sacrifice" (Rom 12:1). A martyr's death in heroic protection of another (others) is indeed an honorable sacrifice. A life lived out in devoted commitment to uplifting and enhancing the benefit of others can be just as surely the "greater love" Jesus describes.

The Incarnation fits this pattern. It was a "living sacrifice" that God made when the Son "emptied himself" of deity to "be born in the likeness of men" (Phil. 2:7). It was "living sacrifice" that Jesus made in a "human life" of living, teaching, helping. Only in his execution did he "lay down" his physical life. In John 10:17-18 Jesus says that "I lay down this life, that I may take it again"—that I have the right and authority (exousian) to both "lay it down, and to take it again." The Passion records in the Gospels tell us that Jesus did "lay down his life" by letting corrupt or evil/power persons kill him. The Easter proclamation, "He is alive," heralds the great victory that human arrogance is vanquished and life triumphs over death through Jesus.

In the Christian fellowship, whenever "love for one another" becomes so real that we care about the well-being of each other as much and even more than our own, we will indeed "spend our lives" in care for and support of each other. Jesus said we will do this if we love each other as he has loved us.

In essence, Jesus tells the disciples: "You are my friends . . . I no longer call you servants . . . I call you friends . . . for I have told you all things (let you in on) . . . all that I have come from the Father to make known unto you."

Jesus reveals the intimately personal kind of relationship that God wants to have with people. Jesus calls the Father Abba during his prayers in Gethsemane, needing the sustaining relation of Father/Son love to help him endure the awesome trial he is facing (see Mark 14:36). The word Abba comes from the Aramaic and is an emphatic form of the usual word for father, Ab.[5] Used as it is in his prayer in combinations with the Greek word Pater, it has the emphasized intimacy of meaning, as in "My Dear Father" (or maybe just "Daddy, Daddy").

Jesus reminds the remaining eleven disciples that they have not come to that relationship with God on the basis of their own merit. He has chosen, trained, and appointed them to "go and bear fruit." Their shared life has caused a relationship between Jesus and them to develop that has "raised" them from servants to friends. In their ongoing lives as they bear fruit that abides, Jesus promises that the same intimacy of relationship will continue with the Father. The harmony will be such that what they ask will please the Father and the Father will give what they ask.

...

CHRISTIAN LIVING IN AN UNFRIENDLY WORLD
(15:18-27)

Jesus talks with the disciples about what they can expect from the world as they go on living and serving after his imminent death. They have learned from him and have come to have faith in and commitment to the truths and values he taught and lived. They are not "of the world" because they will not be living and teaching the ways and values of the world. They can expect to be treated as he has been treated. The world will hate them as the world has hated him.

Jesus is describing what results from people living by different value systems. As people choose how they will live, they develop a life-pattern (and a religious faith) based on what they believe is important. As the old adage says, "Birds of a feather flock together." People like people like themselves, and people tend to be intolerant of people unlike themselves.

The "world," represented by Jewish religious leaders, hates Jesus because he does not "take his place" as an obedient Jew practicing the Mosaic rituals as they interpret them. The disciples will be living by truths and practices learned from Jesus. He tells them "the world" will reject them and persecute them because they do not "know" the Father who has sent him.

The force of the words translated "know" (*oida, eidon, horao*) is more than to merely "have information." Usage spans from "catch sight of," to "perceive/understand," to "experience spiritual perception."[6] Jesus speaks of people who have not come to "know" the character and ways of the Father he reveals.

The Jewish leadership will be successful in their planned "elimination" of Jesus by his death the next day. Jesus promises the disciples, however, that in spite of his "absence" they will not be left without a supporting witness. The Paraclete, Spirit of Truth, will keep the revelation of truth by Jesus alive in the world, along with, and through, the disciples. They are those who have known him and will go on being living witnesses of the light and transforming grace Jesus has brought into the world. Amazingly, Jesus is able to face his imminent death with such positive and hopeful assurances for his disciples. They will have to live through his death and resurrection and go on to be the "followers of the way" and the nucleus of the Christian faith in an unfriendly world.

...

Verses 22-24 raise an authentic moral question. Jesus says that if he had not come and "spoken to them" and "done among them the works" that they (the world) would "not have sin." To understand this statement literally is to believe that "sin" has meaning only in the Christian religion. That kind of religious understanding goes back to the age of tribal polytheism when deities were believed to "possess" lands and "chosen" people.

In that primitive time and religious faith, values and conduct for a specific people had meaning only within that relationship. Everything outside that relationship was the concern of other deities and other people. Since polytheism gave way to monotheism, and God (the Supreme Being) is understood to be the infinite universal Sovereign, the question of moral values and the consequences of moral/immoral actions among people not within the Christian faith is a matter of authentic concern.

Christian believers affirm that "love, joy, peace, patience, ..." are "fruits of the Spirit" (Gal. 5:22) and that "immorality, impurity, licentiousness, ..." do not belong in "the kingdom of God." (Gal. 5:19-21). There are, however, many people who affirm no religious faith but who, nevertheless, choose the high moral values named above and eschew the "works of the flesh."

Consider this as a possible way to believe: God, Designer and Creator, established in the beginning in the very nature of human life the qualities of value and conduct that enhance life, and those that degrade life. Those qualities of life are revealed in the Bible as features in harmony with the character of God. Human persons have the gifted ability to learn by experience, discern the difference, and choose which values and actions to live by. The inescapable consequences of those choices are not believed by many people to be a matter of concern in their lives as they make their day-to-day choices.

The promises of Jesus are certain: The Holy Spirit of God abiding with those who trust God will "teach and bring to remembrance . . . what I (Jesus) have taught you" (John 14:26). One's choices of moral values, and conduct of life by them, are immensely deepened and supported by authentic religious faith. For Christians, that means the presence, help, support, and guidance by God's presence in the Holy Spirit.

...

NEEDED ASSURANCE AND ENCOURAGEMENT
(16:1-4a)

To finish the evening of upper room conversation, Jesus concludes with paragraphs of encouragement for the disciples. He warns them about what to expect as they live as his followers. He tells them his warnings are intended to prepare them so they will not "fall away" in the times of trial to come. They can expect absolute rejection from the Jewish authorities who will drive them out of the synagogues. Their harsh rejection will lead to some adversaries even thinking they are serving God by killing followers of Jesus (note Saul of Tarsus before his conversion in Acts 7:58–9:6). Jesus goes so far as to say that the adversaries among the Jewish leadership have not "known the Father, nor me." There is no clearer statement in our biblical text about the great advance in divine revelation made by Jesus in incarnation over the Jewish comprehension of the nature and character of God. Jesus urges the disciples to remember this when their hours of trauma, uncertainty, and persecution come.

...

The harsh opposition of the Jewish religious leaders to the teachings and practices by Jesus are clear evidence that they considered his revelation and their heritage to be radical opposites.

Jesus says to his followers that they will be rejected by the Jews as he has been rejected, and for the same reason because they, the Jews, "have not known the Father, nor me" (v. 3). Jesus has defined the differences between Jewish religious tenets and his revealed truths to be so fundamental and significant that his followers will need to "remember that I have told you of them" (v. 4).

...

PREPARING THEM FOR HIS ABSENCE
(16:4b-11)

Jesus explains to his disciples why he is telling them things now that he has not told them earlier. While he is with them, they have not needed the warnings and assurances they will surely need now. Their immediate future will be very different from what they have known in the past. The violent end of his life through crucifixion will leave them confused. They have not understood his talk about "going away," and have not asked him for clearer explanation. His statement that he is "going to the one who sent me" has left them troubled and sorrowing. Jesus explains and expands. They will be benefitted by the coming change of Presence. Jesus relates his presence to the presence of the Holy Spirit, describing the role of the Paraclete as ministry of conviction, enlightenment, and discernment through his abiding presence (God with us to guide and enable Christian living).

The Emmanuel/Paraclete promise of God's "presence" has a long history. Isaiah 7:1-16 is a promise of Emmanuel's presence as helping Sovereign in a time of national crisis. Matthew's affirmation about the birth of Jesus is that Immanuel is present in one who will be Savior (1:21-23). On the evening before his death, Jesus promises the coming of a new way of God being present, "another Paraclete," the forever abiding Holy Spirit.

...

There is no record in the text to explain how much of that assurance the disciples grasp and understand, but the truth of the promises becomes real to them at Pentecost and in their ongoing lives. Those promises are strong and abiding assurances for the people of God in all ages.

...

PROMISES ABOUT THE SPIRIT
(16:12-15)

Jesus explains to his disciples that he cannot reveal more to them because they are not yet ready to grasp all the meaning of what is about to happen. He tells them again that the Holy Spirit (the new Paraclete) will play an ongoing vital role in their lives. The Spirit will help them remember and understand what Jesus has taught and done.

The Spirit will be an ongoing Presence with them and will keep on revealing, guiding, and helping them. Jesus emphasizes the unity that exists between Father, Son, *and* Spirit—the oneness that exists within the fullness of God. Where one is, all are; what one is doing, all are doing. Each reveals the fullness of God. Jesus always teaches that there is no differing between the *personas* of God.

FORESIGHT IS NOT EASY
(16:16-24)

The disciples cannot understand the drama of events of the immediate days ahead, events that have not yet happened. They are confused by some of the things Jesus is saying to them to prepare them for what he knows is soon to happen. In these verses their confusion becomes even greater as Jesus says they "will see him no more" and then they "will see him again." The meaning is clear to us because we live after the Crucifixion, the Resurrection events of the following three days, and the "appearances" period. Jesus describes for the disciples the difference the events will mean for them in contrast to what they will mean for "the world." His death will bring sorrow to the disciples but happiness to the world.

Jesus is evidently using "the world" to describe the attitude of the adversary Jewish leaders and the Roman authorities who will be pleased to believe that by his death they have eliminated Jesus as a "thorn in their flesh." Jesus, however, assures the disciples that their sorrow will be turned into joy, referring to his resurrection that will confirm his triumph of life over death. He uses the figure of childbirth, which is rightly called travail (struggle, labor), but that quickly fades into memory in the joy of a new child born. The assurance of his victory over death, which will come to his followers through his "risen and living" appearances, will turn their sense of tragic defeat into an abiding joy. His presence with the Father will transform their prayers.

...

Jesus has foresight that the disciples do not have. Details about the days ahead they cannot yet know. They will need all the assurance Jesus is giving them when they deal with his death and are feeling hopeless. His "victory of life over death" will become for them a recovery of hope and the very foundation of their lives of faith and service. The "triumph of life" that was so vital to those first Christians is also the "ground of faith" for all generations since.

Jesus promised, "because I live, you will live also" (John 14:19). Jesus "presented himself alive" (Acts 1:3) after his physical death. His victory of life over death, spirit over flesh, is the foundation for an assured faith and a sure hope that through God's loving grace our mortality will give way to immortality of spirit at the time of our physical death. As Jesus says, that is a source of joy no one can take from us.

Jesus also describes how his death, resurrection, and ascension will transform their prayer life. "Hitherto" they have not prayed to the Father in his name, for he is present with them and they can ask him directly. "Henceforth" he will not be with them physically, so their prayers will be directed to the Father. Jesus assures them that if they pray to the Father in his name, the Father will hear and respond. This becomes for the disciples an ongoing assurance that the death of Jesus does not leave them "abandoned as orphans" (see John 14:18). The promised presence of the Holy Spirit as the new Paraclete will be the ongoing fulfillment of the Emmanuel (God is with us) tradition that has been at the heart of their faith for centuries.

…

AND NOW, BE AT PEACE
(16:25-33)

So, what does Jesus say in conclusion? He tells the disciples that previously he has used figures of speech to describe things he has been trying to help them understand. The time for figures of speech has passed. His incarnate presence with them is ending. He will now be with the Father, and their fellowship with Father/Son will be as intimate as it has been with him before.

The disciples answer that they are "getting the picture," but Jesus warns them that they do not yet realize what is so soon to happen, and how fearful and traumatic it will be for them. While they will be driven away by fear, he assures them of the Father's presence. He tells his followers again that he is preparing them for tribulation that is sure to come. They can have peace in the confident assurance that he has overcome the world.

Verses 25-33 are John's record of Jesus' last personal words to his disciples. He assures them of the Father's love. He tells them that through his imminent death he is returning to the Father from whom he has come. His last caring words are a warning that trouble is ahead for them. Nevertheless, he encourages them to find peace in the assurance that he has "overcome the world."

…

This summary statement concludes the upper room conversation between Jesus and the disciples that began at 13:31. Jesus has talked intimately and personally with his eleven closest followers. What we have in the text is evidently a record of the evening as it survived in the memory of at least one person who was present, along with the tradition as it was shaped by a generation of early Christians and the inspiration and guidance of the Holy Spirit.

This record includes some of the richest and most treasured expressions that have survived about the character of God, about his active presence and guidance in the lives of people who trust and seek to follow him, and about the hope that sustains and enriches the lives of his people. It reveals, too, some of the greatest insights we have about the purpose and meaning of the incarnation of the Son who reveals God most fully for us. And we have here, also, the most clearly stated promises about the presence and role of the Holy Spirit in the ages after the Incarnation.

The days ahead will bring death for Jesus and tribulation for his followers. But he assures them: "Be of good cheer; I have overcome the world." Those words stand as abiding assurance for everyone whose faith and trust are grounded in God's love and grace.

...

A BENEDICTION BY JESUS
(17:1-5)

All of John 17 stands in the text as a prayer by Jesus. It has been described as a "high priestly" prayer in which Jesus consecrates himself as a perfect sacrifice being offered as an "atoning blood sacrifice," bearing the sins of the world.[7] Jesus begins the prayer with focus on the glory of the Father and the way the Son has revealed that glory (glorified the Father) in his incarnate ministry that is ending. He says that he has "finished/accomplished" (past tense) the work he has come to do. He prays to share again the glory of the Father's presence, that, he affirms, he "had with thee (the Father) before the world was made."

Included in these verses is a central, revealing truth. Jesus defines his incarnate purpose to have been to "give eternal life" to those who were given to be his. He defines "eternal life" as "to know the only true God" and himself as the one "whom thou hast sent."

These verses raise again for us the meaning of "glory" and "glorify" as they are used in the Fourth Gospel (see the commentary section of John 12:20-36a). In these verses, glory/glorify seems clearly to refer to the divine majesty that belongs innately to their character as Father and Son.

Jesus affirms that the central purpose of his incarnation has been to make eternal life a reality for all who belong to God, "all whom thou hast given him (me)" (v. 2). He defines what eternal life means: "that they may know thee the only true God, and Jesus Christ whom thou hast sent" (v. 3). He prays about his return to the glory he shares with the Father from the eternal past, (the "equality with God" he laid aside when he "emptied himself, taking the form of a servant, being born in the likeness of men"—see Phil. 2:5-8). Having "accomplished the work" of incarnation, his need for living in human physical limitations is completed.

The focus of this prayer's beginning is on the relationship of the Son with the Father and the fulfilled purpose of the incarnation. The remainder of the prayer focuses on the disciples, his preparation of them to be ongoing witnesses, and their consecration for ministry in an unfriendly world.

...

JESUS PRAYS FOR HIS DISCIPLES
(17:6-19)

Jesus talks with the Father about his now completed ministry among the disciples. Jesus has revealed the Father to the disciples. They have received what he has revealed, believed its truth, and "kept his (thy) word." At this crucial time Jesus says that he is praying for his followers specifically, not for the world at large. They are his witnesses, they reveal his glory, and they will need a new channel of guidance and help—for he will be with them physically no longer. Jesus prays about the way they have become his followers and now they are hated by the world because they are like him. Jesus asks not that they be taken out of the world but that as they live and serve they will be kept secure from evil. As he sends them into the world, Jesus prays for their consecration "in truth."

This portion of the prayer focuses on the departure of Jesus from his group of followers, and on what he has accomplished among them in the ministry of his incarnation. Jesus affirms that he has done what he came to do. His task is finished, he is coming "home" to the Father, so he prays for his followers that their faith will continue steadfast and the unity that has developed with him will be ongoing among them (vv. 11-13).

His followers are not of the world any longer because they have come to believe in him and trust the truth he has revealed to them. The next day the "world" will kill Jesus, and his followers will be in fear of their lives because they are his, and like him they "are not of the world." Jesus prays that while they are "in the world" but not "of the world," they will be guarded and guided, maintaining their unity, and being blessed with joy as they live out the mission to which he is sending them.

JESUS PRAYS FOR CHRISTIANS UNIVERSALLY
(17:20-26)

In the last section of the prayer Jesus expands to universal the intended reach and purpose of his incarnation. He prays for all who will come to believe in him through the witness of those who have become his followers through his life and teachings. Jesus describes the intention of God in the Incarnation as the beginning of the gospel, that generation after generation of believers will share the gospel, "so that the world may believe that thou hast sent me" (v. 21).

Jesus prays for a unity and spirit of love to develop and prevail among all who believe and belong. The pattern he describes is the eternal unity and love of God, Father, Son, and Spirit. Jesus prays for unselfish, outreaching, caring love of God that includes all of humankind. This is the love that caused God to choose incarnate self-revelation as a means to express his love and reconcile sinful persons into a fellowship of harmony with himself.

In conclusion (v. 24), Jesus describes the eternal focus of this fellowship of love and harmony. He prays that all who belong to him through faith and trust will be with him and the Father. This prayer defines a hope for Christians beyond mortal life in immortal spirit. Jesus vows an unending "making known" of God's love that is the ongoing bond of unity between humankind and God.

...

Jesus prays for those who will become the body of Christians ("those who are to believe in me through their word"), who in generations to follow gather into Christian churches. And he prays about the future of them all, that they may share the unity of God and ultimately the presence of God in the realm of eternal spirit (". . . be with me where I am . . . "). The expressed goal of his incarnate life, and now his prayer for them, is that his followers with have God's love in them and "I in them." This prayer we cherish, believing it includes us also.

...

NOTES

[1] William Barclay, *The Gospel of John, vol. 2* (Philadelphia: Westminster Press, 1956), 167-171.

[2] G. Abbott-Smith, *A Manual Greek Lexicon of the New Testament, 3rd ed.* (Edinburgh: T& TClark, 1950), 3-4, 469-470.

[3] Ibid., 445, 457.

[4] William F. Arndt and F. Wilbur Gingrich, eds., *Walter Bauer's, Greek-English Lexicon of the New Testament, 2nd ed.,* (Chicago: University of Chicago Press, 1979), 893-894.

[5] Abbott-Smith, *Lexicon,* 1.

[6] Arndt and Gingrich, *Bauer's Lexicon,* 220, 555, 577-578.

[7] Wilbert F. Howard, "The Gospel According to St. John, Exegesis," *The Interpreter's Bible, vol. 8* (New York: Abingdon Press, 1952), 742.

Arrogant Power in Action
(John 18:1–19:42)

GETHSEMANE
(18:1-11)

In the first verses of John 18 we have the account of the Gethsemane event. Unlike the Synoptic Gospels, John does not record the Gethsemane prayers. But John does include the record of the longer prayer found in chapter 17, which is not included in any of the Synoptics. All four gospels record the betrayal by Judas, but John does not include the traitor's kiss as a part of his identification. John does include a longer conversation between Jesus and the band of soldiers and officers.

In this conversation Jesus identifies himself as the person they are seeking, apparently amazing them with the freedom of his admission. Jesus, in turn, asks that the disciples be allowed to leave without any charges. Luke writes that the disciples ask Jesus if they should fight for him. Matthew and Luke record that "one of them" draws a sword. John writes that it is Simon Peter who strikes the high priest's servant and cuts off his ear. Jesus tells them to stop, for he will "drink the cup" of consequences for the opposition that has arisen because of what he has done and taught in his incarnate life and ministry.

...

> *The reference to "cup" here is understood to mean "crucifixion as substitute blood sacrifice" in traditional interpretations of this passage. This is too limited a meaning, however. The divine gift and human consequence of incarnation are much larger than the execution death of Jesus will be. The Incarnation involves emptying of divine status, becoming human, revealing truths about God and humanity by life and teaching, enduring accusation and opposition by the most influential leaders of fellow Jews, and ultimately being killed by their scheming and manipulation.*
>
> *The "cup" Jesus will drink is the "consequences" of his incarnation. The consequence of his death and resurrection is that the evil of human arrogance and drive for power is exposed and vanquished and the victory of life over death is made a sure hope for humanity. Jesus will pay an inestimable price for an eternal victory on the behalf of his followers. For the joy that is set before him, he will endure the cross (Heb. 12:2).*

...

THE BEGINNING OF TRIALS
(18:12-14)

After arresting Jesus, the soldiers take him to the Jewish authorities who had sent them to arrest and bring Jesus. They take him first to Annas, the father-in-law of the high priest Caiaphas. In his role as high priest and chief officer of the Sanhedrin, Caiaphas has earlier declared that it is "expedient that one man should die for the people that the whole nation should not perish" (John 11:49-52). His statement reveals the strategy of the Jewish leaders to eliminate Jesus to avoid carnage by the Roman military to put down turmoil within the Jewish nation.

Apparently Annas is the "power behind the throne." For much of Jewish history the high-priesthood has been an inherited position with lifelong tenure. The Romans apparently do not want any one person to have that degree of influence, so they require the office to rotate. The family of Annas is wealthy and influential, so they are able to keep the office rotating among themselves

---

SIMON PETER'S DENIAL
(18:15-18, 25-27)

Simon Peter reveals his personal disposition by his actions in the face of the arrest of Jesus. He is an impulsive man, acting on his first thought, often having to take back his words or change his position. He shows his devotion to Jesus, however, by staying close enough to learn what will happen. His care-to-know leads him to follow to the court of the high priest where the soldiers take Jesus. "Another disciple" (believed by many to be John) also goes along. This other disciple is known personally by some of the "insiders," for he is readily admitted into the court. Peter is kept outside until the other disciple asks the doorkeeper to let him into the court.

Peter's entrance into the palace court puts him into a position that leads to his embarrassment and to his later distress. First the maid at the door, and later a servant by the fire, recognizes Peter well enough to question him about his relationship with Jesus. He, who is daring enough to follow Jesus into the palace court, proves not to be courageous enough to admit who he really is. Peter denies three times that he is a follower of Jesus. As Jesus has warned him, when he hears the cock crow, he is smitten with guilt, he goes out, and weeps bitterly (see Matt. 26:75).

...

By Jewish ritual law, male chickens are not permitted to be kept in Jerusalem, and also when a rooster will crow is a very undeterminable time. But there is a very set time every night. By Roman military rule, the "fourth watch" for the changing of

the guard happens at 3:00 am and is signaled by a trumpet blast from the central Praetorian guardhouse and heard throughout the city. That trumpet blast is locally called "the cockcrow," announcing the approaching dawn. It does not change the meaning of the event described in scripture, but it may well be that the trumpet signaling the fourth watch of the night is the "cockcrow" that Peter hears, and it happens before the night ends—just as Jesus has warned Peter.[1]

...

THE JEWISH TRIAL
(18:19-24,28)

Inside the palace, the trial of Jesus is underway, with the first questioning done by Annas. Jesus refuses to defend himself, but replies to Annas' accusing questions by admitting that he has taught openly, so they can easily find witnesses to what he had said and done. An officer strikes Jesus and berates him for the way he answers the priest. Jesus does not give in. When Annas sees he is not gaining the desired evidence, he sends Jesus on to Caiaphas. The Synoptic Gospels all record more extensive questioning of Jesus and consultation by the Sanhedrin among themselves. They are already determined that Jesus must die. John simply records that they take Jesus on to be tried by Pilate.

...

Note in the records of trial that Jesus does not behave like a submissive "lamb led to the slaughter." He neither hesitates nor defends himself. He declares what he has done as his evidence of who he is. He yields to those in authority and lets them kill him. In doing so he exposes their corrupt evil and vanquishes them by his living victory.

...

EVASIVE PLOTTING
(18:28-32)

John alone records that the Jews will not go into the Roman buildings because to do so will cause them to be ritually unclean and consequently prohibited from eating the Passover meal when the Sabbath begins at six o'clock that evening. Pilate questions the Jews outside about their case against Jesus and the verdict they want. Inside he questions Jesus.

The Jews obviously do not want to have to make their case against Jesus. Pilate tells them to just deal with Jesus with the level of authority they have within their Jewish law. The Jews want Jesus dead, but the Romans will not allow them the authority to execute him. Verse 32 is an interpretation by the writer that Roman execution is necessary; crucifixion is the means by which Jesus must die.

> The Jewish method of execution is stoning (Lev. 20:10, John 8:5), but the Romans use crucifixion as their most cruel and dehumanizing form of execution—primarily for slaves, the lowest rank of criminals, and political criminals.² Roman citizens are exempt, however. (According to tradition, Paul, a Roman citizen, was beheaded.)
>
> The interpretative statement in verse 32, that crucifixion is the necessary way Jesus must die, is based on a specific tenet of faith. God, by design, destined the death of Jesus to be a substitutionary, ritual, blood-atoning sacrifice to pay the penalty for the offense of human sinfulness of which all humankind is believed to be guilty because of the original sin of Adam and Eve.

...

I do not understand the gospel records of the death of Jesus in this way. Two Synoptic Gospels record that in the wilderness temptation Jesus chooses not to use control over people (join up with the devil) as the way he will accomplish his redemptive reconciling mission of incarnation (Matt. 4:8-10, Luke 4:5-8).

Jesus teaches and practices a different meaning for religion than that of ritual legalism. He sets forth a "salvation" based on personal life transformation through human "faith and repentance" and divine "forgiveness and reconciliation." Jesus challenges both the teaching and the authority of the Jewish leadership. He comes to Jerusalem to challenge the principle of "power as the way to make people right with God."

The Jewish power structure, the religious and political establishment alike, manipulates his death to eliminate Jesus as a threat to them and their authority; he has taught and practiced that greatness is in service. Too much of humanity has still not learned the lesson that true greatness is measured in doing the most good, not in gaining positions of influence and heaps of wealth and privilege for oneself.

...

THE ROMAN TRIAL
(18:33-40)

Pilate questions Jesus about whether he claims to be a king. To Pilate, the Jews are charging Jesus with being a ruler (a political charge) instead of a blasphemer, claiming to be a Son of God (a religious charge). They know that Pilate does not care about their religious disagreements, so they turn to political scheming.

Jesus answers Pilate respectfully with a question, asking about the source of any evidence the governor has. Pilate replies that the charges have come from the Jewish people. The next reply by Jesus states, but does not explain, the difference between a political area of rule (imposed control, "of this world"), and a spiritual realm of sovereignty (embraced devotion, "not of this world"). Jesus is talking about something that has no meaning to Pilate.

The governor replies, "So you are a king." Jesus explains, "You say I am a king," i.e. you think in terms of political authority and control over people. Jesus describes his role in the world as something entirely different. He says he has come to reveal "truth" as light for people so they can choose what to believe and how to live. Pilate is befuddled, but he raises an enormously important question: "What is truth?" He receives no answer. Pilate is convinced, however, that Jesus is no political revolutionary and represents no threat of insurrection against Rome.

Pilate goes out and announces his decision to the Jewish crowd. He offers, in hope of pacifying the crowd, to fulfill a Passover custom and release Jesus. He cannot offer a less acceptable proposal to them, however. They yell instead for the release of a robber, Barabbas.

ATTEMPTED NEGOTIATION
(19:1-11)

The battle of determined minds has not ended. Pilate is convinced that Jesus is no threat to Roman civil order. The Jewish leadership is determined to get Jesus killed. Pilate hopes he can appease the Jewish crowd by punishing Jesus with something less than death. He has Jesus scourged. Along with the severe beating, the Roman soldiers mock and abuse Jesus.

Pilate presents Jesus before the crowd and declares him not guilty of any Roman crime: "Here is the man." Jesus stands there, beaten almost to death and wearing the mocking crown of thorns and a royal robe. Pilate's declaration seems to imply, "This is what I think of your 'king,' but for your pleasure I have had him beaten because he has offended you."

The Jewish leaders begin to yell for his crucifixion. Pilate mocks them with the suggestion that they crucify him themselves, knowing that they are not authorized to do it. The Jews, having failed to get Jesus killed as a political revolutionary, try to use their religious claim that he should die for being a blasphemer, claiming to be a Son of God.

Their change in tactics causes Pilate enough concern that he takes Jesus back inside and questions him further. He asks, "Where are you from?" To that question Jesus gives him no answer. Pilate asks Jesus if he does not recognize his authority over him. Jesus tells Pilate that he would have no authority had he not received it "from above." There is no indication whether "from above" means "from God" or "from appointment by higher Roman authority." His following declaration is that the Jewish leaders ("those who have delivered me to you") are the real source of the trouble and therefore guilty of the greater sin.

INTIMIDATION
(19:12-16)

Pilate wants to release Jesus, but the Jews will not allow it if they can find a way to prevent it. They turn to intimidation, threatening to report Pilate to the emperor for allowing a possible revolutionary to act like a king without Roman approval. Pilate cannot take that risk, so he bows to their demands. He brings Jesus out before the crowd, takes his seat on the official judgment seat, and declares his verdict: "Here is your king!"

The crowd, now a mob, yells for Jesus' death. The chief priests declare for their nation, "We have no king but Caesar," a declaration that must gall them to the depths of their souls. Pilate consigns Jesus to death by crucifixion. Matthew's gospel (27:24-26) records that Pilate washes his hands, and declares himself innocent of the miscarriage of justice that is happening. The gathered Jewish crowd, having been incited by their leaders, answer "His blood be on us and on our children." So, Barabbas is released and Jesus is sentenced to die.

> According to recorded evidence, Jesus is tried by Jews in the early hours of Friday (14 Nissan), condemned by Pilate and crucified sometime about midmorning, dies about midafternoon, and is entombed before sundown (the beginning of 15 Nissan, the Passover Sabbath). There is significant agreement that John is correct that Friday is the "day of preparation" and that Jesus is crucified on the day the sacrificial Passover lambs are slaughtered. The most unreconciled item in records about that day has to do with the hour of crucifixion.
>
> Both Jews and Romans divide days into hours of darkness and hours of light. Both begin to count daylight hours from dawn.[3] Mark records the hour of crucifixion as the "third" hour, 9:00 a.m. (15:25). No other gospel records an hour for the crucifixion. All three Synoptics record the same "hours of darkness" from six till nine, noon till 3:00 p.m. (Matt. 27:45, Mark 15:33, Luke 23:44). The records in the Fourth Gospel agree with the Synoptics that the Jewish trials occur in the night or early dawn (John 18:13, 19, 27) and that Jesus is taken before Pilate "early" (John 18:28). Then John records that it is the "sixth" hour (12 noon) before Pilate condemns Jesus and sends him forth to be crucified (John 19:14-16). John records that Jesus dies and is entombed before the end of the day and the beginning of the Sabbath (John 19:31, 42). The times recorded in John allow for less than six hours from crucifixion to death and entombment. Crucifixion normally means long hours of agonizing suffering, sometimes a full day or longer, before a victim will die. (There must have developed an error in the Fourth Gospel account of times during later generations of copying.)
>
> Some Christians have difficulty reconciling another matter of timing in the Passion events. When Jesus speaks of his death, he says that he will rise "after three days" (Mark 8:31), or "on the third day" (Matt. 16:22, Luke 9:22). In one record, however, Jesus uses Jonah as a "sign" and, by comparison,

says that "the Son of Man will be three days and three nights in the heart of the earth" (Matt. 12:40). Those who believe the story of Jonah to be an historical event instead of an inspired parable, and who take the words of Matthew's account to be intended literally, consequently have a problem with the traditional understanding of the Passion events' timing.

Jesus is in the tomb at most only a few hours of Friday before sundown, all of Friday night, all of Saturday, and some hours after sundown Saturday before dawn on Sunday. (The Gospels give no record about when Jesus "arose," simply that the disciples find the tomb empty on Easter morning.) There are no records in the Passion accounts that establish more than part of one day, all of one night, all of one day, and part of one night. Even if we count part of a day or night a whole day or night, the records account for two days and two nights. Those who try to reconcile the Passion accounts with the Jonah comparison interpret the Passion records to begin a day earlier with the last supper on Wednesday night and the crucifixion on Thursday morning. The reference by Jesus is about "signs."

As Jonah was a "sign" to Israel that God loved Ninevites just as he loved Israelites, the Son of Man will be a "sign" to all people that those who trust in the love and grace of God will be victorious over death just as Jesus is. There seems to be no reason to be concerned about the variance in numbers of hours and days.

CRUCIFIXION
(19:17-22)

"They" (v. 17) evidently includes both the angry Jewish mob and the military detail that is assigned the task of execution. There is an established place of execution, a hill having the shape of a skull. Its location is not known. Two other men, condemned criminals, are also crucified. A written sign is placed on the cross, identifying Jesus and stating the "crime" for which he is being executed. The Jewish priests object to the wording. Pilate denies their request for change in the wording.

The traditional site of crucifixion and entombment, the Church of the Holy Sepulcher, was established in the fourth century through the influence of Emperor Constantine and his mother Helen. A tradition about the location of the crucifixion is reflected in Hebrews 13:12, "So Jesus also suffered outside the gate," and in John 19:20, "The place where Jesus was crucified was near the city." Which wall? Which gate? There is no definite answer.

The site of the crucifixion is outside the city, according to the records in Hebrews and John. Crucifixion is a Roman means of execution. Jews would consider it ritually defiling to the city, and would raise violent objections if it were done inside the city. The site is alongside a road leading out of the city. Romans place crosses along roads for maximum exposure to gain as much deterrence as possible for anyone who might be inclined to unlawful actions.

There is unsolvable uncertainty about the location of the Second Wall of Jerusalem, built in the early Herodian period. No archaeological remains have been found to determine its location, so its actual path in the city is not known. That uncertainty affects the question of the correctness of the Holy Sepulcher Church as the site of Golgotha. Evidence for the more modern claims about Gordon's Calvary and the Garden Tomb are not convincing as the site of the crucifixion, though the area "feels" more appropriate than the congestion of the Holy Sepulcher Church site.

The writing placed above Jesus' head is meant to be the charge for which a condemned person is being executed. The statement is a declaration, and the Jews want it to read as a claim by Jesus. Pilate responds to their complaint and refuses to change the statement. He stands by what he has written, as much as to say to them, "He really was the best of your crowd."

DIVIDING HIS CLOTHES
(19:23-25a)

The four soldiers who crucify the three men divide Jesus' garments among themselves. They choose to cast lots for his tunic instead of ripping it apart. None of the gospels record whether or not they also divide any personal items from the other two men. We can assume that they did. It is widely reported that this division of clothing by the soldiers is a Roman custom, a "perk" for having to do the unpleasant task of execution. John, however, interprets it as a fulfillment of prophetic foretelling in Psalm 22:18.

THE LAST LINGERING FAITHFUL
(19:25b-27)

The Gospels record that a group of Jesus' followers, mostly women, gather and watch the crucifixion (Matt. 27:56, Mark 15:40, Luke 23:49, John 19:25). Four of them and at least one man, believed to be John, are named as standing near the cross. They are Mary (the mother of Jesus), Salome (Mary's sister, the mother of James and John the sons of Zebedee), Mary (wife of Clopas and the mother of James and Joses, about whom there is no other information), and Mary Magdalene.

John alone includes the beautiful account of Jesus committing his mother to "the disciple whom he loved," and asking him to care for Mary as if she were his own mother.

Interpreters differ about why those who stay near the cross dare to be there while the disciples have fled. It seems reasonable to assume that among the larger crowd that apparently is present, the soldiers have little interest in anything except their execution assignment. The predominance of women among them makes it less likely they would be considered possible insurgents.

An interesting aside about the presence of Jesus' mother near the cross: Mary is mentioned only twice in John's gospel—at the marriage in Cana in John 2:1-5 and in this passage. The sensitivity of Jesus to care about his mother at this critical moment of both their lives is touching indeed, and we are indebted to John for preserving it for us.

DEATH RECORDS
(19:28-30)

The Synoptic Gospels record that before the crucifixion the soldiers offer Jesus drugged wine, but he refuses to drink it (Matt. 27:33-34, Mark 15:22-23). The Gospels all record sayings by Jesus from the cross (seven total, but none recorded in all four gospels). As death approaches, John records that Jesus says "I thirst" and does drink the vinegar offered. Then, in affirmation that he has accomplished his mission, he says simply, "It is finished." Then he bows his head and welcomes death.

DEATH RITUALS
(19:31-37)

Men hanging on crosses create a problem for the Jewish leaders. In Jewish tradition an executed criminal who is hanged on a tree is accursed by God and must not hang overnight, for that would defile the land (Deut. 21:23). Paul interprets this to mean that crucifixion makes Jesus accursed (Gal. 3:13). The ritual concerns of the Jews cause them to have an urgent need to hasten the deaths of the condemned and get them off the crosses before sundown when the Sabbath will begin.

They request Pilate to have the legs of the crucified broken so the "criminals" will die quickly and can be removed. Since Jesus is already dead, there is no reason to break his legs. One of the soldiers does thrust a spear into his side, however. The writer adds a "fulfillment of prophecy" explanation of what has happened.

The approaching night is of special concern to the Jewish leaders because the day of preparation is ending and the Passover Sabbath will begin at sundown.

The request to Pilate to have the legs of the crucified ones broken is meant to make those persons unable to resist the full effects of hanging suspended on crosses. They will die more quickly. The soldier who thrusts a spear into Jesus' side appears to do it almost as an afterthought, as if to say, "It's over—good riddance."

John gives a prophetic interpretation. He cites Exodus 12:46 that "no bone of a Passover lamb is to be broken," and Zechariah 12:10 that "they shall look on him whom they have pierced," a reference apparently to an unknown martyr's death. He has earlier (v. 28) cited the statement, "I thirst," as a fulfilment of Psalm 69:21.

...

Citations of New Testament events as fulfillment of Old Testament records are sometimes problematic. Such citations reflect the familiarity of the Old Testament documents by the New Testament writers, and the esteem in which those documents are held as sacred. At times, however, the context and meaning of the Old Testament event are significantly different from the context and meaning of the New Testament event. The effect of context on the meaning of an event is so important, it seems that responsible biblical study and interpretation require context always to be taken into account and applied.

...

ENTOMBMENT
(19:38-42)

Joseph and Nicodemus take on the compassionate ministry of caring for the dead body of Jesus. Joseph obtains permission from Pilate and takes the body from the cross. Nicodemus joins him and provides spices. They wrap the body with spices in linen cloths and place it in a nearby new tomb.

The Jewish officials are concerned to hasten the executed men's death. They will have nothing to do with the disposition of any dead body, however, because it will make them ritually unclean and they will be prohibited from eating the Passover that evening (Lev. 21:1-5; Num. 5:1-3, 19:11). Roman practices differ for disposing of dead bodies.

Bodies of executed criminals are left on crosses as deterrent warnings. Scavengers eventually devour them. Some bodies are given to family members for disposal. Others are dumped in the garbage fires of Hinom. Joseph's request and Pilate's permission make possible the honorable entombment of Jesus' body.

Joseph of Arimathea is described as a rich man (Matt. 27:57) and a member of the Sanhedrin Council (Mark 15:42, Luke 23:50), but a secret disciple of Jesus (Matt. 27:57, John 19:38). The town of Arimathea is of uncertain location. There is no reference to it except its association with Joseph. His official status makes it possible for him to get to Pilate to request authority to "take away" the body of Jesus.

The Synoptic Gospels record that Joseph does the burial alone. John records that Nicodemus, a fellow Council member and also a secret disciple, comes forward to help Joseph and furnishes spices to be wrapped with the body. Jewish custom, for those wealthy enough to provide, is to wrap a dead body in linen shroud with embalming spices wrapped into the folds of the shroud. Joseph and Nicodemus place the body in a new tomb

(Matthew records that it is Joseph's own that he has carved in rock) and roll a stone to cover the entrance.

The tomb is conveniently located near the place of the crucifixion, so they are able to complete the entombment before sundown. Apparently, Joseph and Nicodemus have no concern about becoming defiled by handling the body of Jesus. Luke has a concluding comment that they rest on the Sabbath.

NOTES

[1] William Barclay, *The Gospel of John, vol. 2* (Philadelphia: Westminster Press, 1956), 268-69.

[2] S. Vernon McCasland, "New Testament Times," *The Interpreter's Bible, vol. 7* (New York: Abingdon Press, 1951), 83.

[3] Michal Hunt, "Agape Bible Study" (web search 2012); Wikipedia, "Roman Timekeeping," (web search).

Assurance, Hope, Guidance
(John 20:1–21:25)

Two nights and a day have passed since the burial of Jesus. Matthew records that the Jewish Council and leading Pharisees have been busy (27:62-66). On the day after the day of preparation (it is the Passover Sabbath, but that does not deter them), the Jewish chief priests and leading Pharisees go to Pilate and request the tomb be sealed and a guard set to make it secure. They claim to fear that the disciples will steal the body and perpetrate a fraud that Jesus has arisen from the dead. Pilate grants their request but seems to add a bit of scorn by saying, "Make it as secure as you can."

Before sundown on Friday, after watching the entombment, the women prepare spices for burial (Luke 23:56). They apparently are not aware of the degree to which Joseph and Nicodemus have shrouded the body on Friday afternoon. They plan to do a more proper completion of burial after the Sabbath. The followers of Jesus observe the Sabbath properly by resting (Luke 23:54-56).

Early on Sunday morning some of the women begin to return to the tomb. John names Mary Magdalene. Matthew names Mary Magdalene and the other Mary (probably the mother of James and Joses). Mark names Magdalene, Mary the mother of James, and Salome the mother of Zebedee's sons. Luke refers to the women who bought and prepared spices for shrouding the body. All of them find the tomb empty.

The disciples are faced with the incredible mystery of death and the reality of the empty tomb. The only attempt in the Gospels to explain the absence of the physical body is that Jesus has "arisen."

Mary Magdalene reacts to her discovery of the empty tomb by going hurriedly to report that fact to Simon Peter and "the other disciple." Simon Peter and John run to the tomb and also find it empty. They return to their homes, still mystified. John records that what Jesus has said about "rising from the dead" has not yet become real for them.

Mary Magdalene returns to the tomb. The Fourth Gospel alone has the recorded tradition of Mary lingering near the tomb and experiencing a personal "resurrection appearance" by Jesus. The account reflects the mystery about "resurrection appearances." The bodily form of the appearance is such that Mary does not recognize Jesus, believing him to be the gardener, until he speaks her name. The tradition recorded here has Jesus say to Mary, "Do not hold me for I have not yet ascended." Mary Magdalene goes and shares with the others about her experience.

I have not found convincing certainty about what the reference to "hold me" means. The three Greek texts I checked all have the same form of the word *APTO*. This basic verb is variously used to mean: to kindle a fire, to come into contact with, to touch, to take hold of, and to cling to. Does Jesus mean ...

- "Don't touch me because it would be confusing to you since I am no longer physical"?
- "Don't hold onto me and delay me" for I "have not yet ascended" but "I am ascending"?
- Don't cling to me to keep from being afraid"?

Why would Jesus say to Mary, "Don't touch me" when eight days later the risen Christ will say to Thomas, "put your hand into my side" (John 20:27), and to the disciples, "it is I myself, handle me, and see (Luke 24:39)"? What did Jesus mean, and why?

...

It is significant that none of the gospel writers attempt to describe a resurrection event, or to define the time when Jesus "leaves the tomb." I take seriously the tradition recorded in Luke 23:43 that Jesus says to the repentant criminal, "Today you will be with me in Paradise." I understand this to mean that at the moment of physical death (on Friday) the "soul" (the spirit person) goes immediately into the spirit realm of existence to "go on living, beatifically" in the presence and care of God. This, in turn, leads me to believe that all Joseph and Nicodemus place in the tomb on Friday is the physical body of Jesus. The tenet about Jesus preaching "to the saints in prison" (1 Pet. 3:19) is not based on a teaching by Jesus.

There are many unanswerable questions for us in the recorded traditions about the Resurrection and events in the days following. Two things have such certainty that they are foundational for our Christian faith, however:

1. *Jesus was not annihilated by physical death. Physical death affects only his physical body. His incarnate life, physical death, and spiritual victory over death are a wonderful witness and assurance that we are spiritual persons who live a physical life and survive physical death in immortal life in the realm of spirit with God.*
2. *After his physical death, for their benefit, Jesus makes himself known to his disciples in appearances to assure them that he is indeed still victoriously alive.*

This reality is difficult for the disciples to believe. They have a lot to process and deal with. They have to decide what is the meaning of this reality for themselves and their lives. The Scriptures contain a thread of revelation and developing spiritual awareness that is important and enlightening here. It is a truth that these first Christians have to come to believe. It is what I call the awesome Immanuel/ Paraclete truth about God: God is with us, and God is on our side for life and for good. This kind of faith sustains the disciples as they go on to live as the first Christians, and to become the nucleus of the developing Christian church.

...

RESURRECTION "APPEARANCES"
(20:19-29)

Luke and John have more details about resurrection appearances than do Matthew and Mark. Luke has the Emmaus Road record, the detail about Jesus eating broiled fish, and his instruction for the disciples to wait in Jerusalem for the coming of the Holy Spirit. Both Luke and John tell of the appearance to the disciple group on the evening of Resurrection Day. Both record that Jesus calls attention to his hands and side as evidence that it is indeed him alive.

John has the distinctive detail that Jesus blesses the disciples with peace, commissions them to be witnesses, and breathes on them the gift of the Holy Spirit. John also tells of Thomas' inability to believe until he has seen Jesus for himself. Jesus adds an assuring word about blessing for all who will believe without the privilege of seeing.

Verse 23 raises a question for us. This statement about "forgiving or retaining sins" corresponds to the statement by Jesus to Simon Peter in Matthew 16:19 about "binding or loosing on earth." These two passages are the only places in the Gospels where I find there is reference to people "absolving" other people of sins. Other references to people forgiving are about our forgiving trespasses or offenses against us, not about forgiving sin. Both Mark 2:7-10 and Luke 5:21-24 record the established belief that only God can forgive sin.

Some interpreters seek to resolve this apparent conflict by citing the grammatical form of the phrases "are forgiven" and "are retained." Both Greek words are in the perfect indicative passive, which have the effect of saying that the forgiving is a thing that is done in the past and is over and done with.[1] This understanding of the statement by Jesus means that the disciples will be affirming a forgiveness by God already done. I do not find this to be persuasive.

...

Early development of Christian theology does not reflect a belief in or practice of forgiving or retaining/binding or loosing of sin by the apostles. As early as CE 97–100, forgiveness came to be associated with baptism. In the mandates of the Pastor of Hermas it is written, "There is no other repentance than this, that we go down into the water and receive forgiveness of our past sins."[2]

As the organized church developed a more hierarchal structure (Council of Arles, CE 316), forgiveness became identified with the rituals of Baptism and the Lord's Supper as sacraments, gifts of God administered by clergy.[3]

By the time of the Council of Trent (1545–1563), Catholic doctrine had added the "Sacrament of Penance" and "Absolution of Sins committed since baptism" as established tenets of faith. Absolution is, in Catholic doctrine, an act of a priest as "a competent authority" to free a penitent of sin. The act of absolution presupposes on the part of the penitent "contrition, confession, and promise of satisfaction." These features of forgiveness as tenets of faith are based in Catholic doctrine on the biblical passages of Matthew 16:18-19 and John 20:23.[4] *The authority for absolution is believed to be based on forgiveness as a sacramental gift of God and the priest as a competent administrator of the sacrament (with the priest becoming "competent" through ordination received from the successive line of bishops since Simon Peter).*

I find no evidence that either of these passages in Matthew or John is in fact a later "copyist addition." The difference from other New Testament records about forgiveness of sin and the later practice of "priestly absolution of sin" seem to point to tenets developed later by priestly hierarchy.

…

"DOUBTING" THOMAS
(20:26-29)

A week later Jesus appears to the disciples again, and this time Thomas is present. Jesus talks with Thomas personally, showing his hands and side, and encouraging Thomas to "be not faithless, but believing." Jesus concludes with a summary statement that is vitally important for all of us. He asks Thomas, "Have you believed BECAUSE you have seen me?" Then he states a truth for all humankind, "Blessed are those who have not seen and yet believe."

…

People have always had a problem with how to understand, describe, and relate to the realm of spirit that is a nonphysical and therefore nonvisible realm. In our physical lives we have no difficulty believing in gravity, heat, cold, and so on because we experience them with our physical senses. In the realm of religion and faith the same is not true. The soul (spirit) is not a material entity, and therefore we are not able to "sense" it with physical senses.

People have always attributed human characteristics to the deities (God/gods) they believe in and worship. We have no other language to use to describe them. People believe their deities want to embody themselves in material objects to find habitation and become an entity. Developing religions carved idol images and worshipped heavenly bodies, natural objects, and animals as habitations of deities. Many Christians believe that God chooses to embody himself in bread and wine in order to convey sacramental grace to his people.

Jesus implies by his statement to Thomas and the gathered disciples that spiritual realities are sufficient in themselves to enable faith, trust, and commitment of life. All who believe in love, grace, trust, and eternal life (non-material realities) bear witness by our faith that we believe what Jesus promised, and we are blessed.

...

CONCLUDING SUMMARY
(20:30-31)

The summary verses of John 20 give every indication that the writer is concluding this gospel. He affirms the far greater and more extensive ministry of Jesus and declares his purpose for the writing he has done.

ANOTHER RESURRECTION "APPEARANCE"
(21:1-3)

John 21 is often described as an epilogue. The summary at the end of chapter 20 indicates a first conclusion to this gospel. When this additional resurrection "appearance" happens in the sequence of events is not certain. It is described in verse 14 as the third time Jesus appears to the disciples. His arrival in Galilee evidently comes after the appearances in Judea in the days immediately following the Resurrection. In numbering, the writer seems to distinguish between appearances to groups of disciples and an individual appearance to Mary Magdalene (John 20:11-17) and to the two disciples in Emmaus (Luke 24:13-31). In this instance there are seven disciples together. Other appearances are referred to in Matthew 28:16-17 and 1 Corinthians 15:5-8.

Simon Peter declares his intent to go fishing. The other six disciples agree to go with him. Through the night they catch nothing.

...

A question is raised here that is not answered in the text. Is Simon Peter saying that their venture of following Jesus is now done with and he is going back to the life of work he followed before going about with Jesus? We cannot tell, but this is surely the kind of questioning and decision-making the disciples have to work out for themselves after Jesus is no longer with them physically.

...

THE MORNING "CATCH"
(21:4-14)

Near dawn, after a unproductive night, the disciples are "calling it quits" and nearing their docking place. Jesus stands on the beach, but as with Mary Magdalene at the tomb and the two disciples on the road to Emmaus, the disciples do not recognize him. While they are still at some distance from shore, Jesus calls and asks if they have "anything to eat," inquiring whether they have caught any fish. They answer "No," and are told to cast the net again on the right side of their boat. They do, and net more fish than they can haul into the boat.

At the wonder of the event, John recognizes it is Jesus who has spoken, and says so to Peter. Then, Peter puts on a garment and jumps from the boat to swim or wade ashore. The other disciples come ashore in the boat, dragging the net full of fish. The distance is about a hundred yards.

The statement "he was naked" (KJV)/"stripped for work" (RSV) has been interpreted both "that he was naked" and "that he had stripped off his tunic down to a less-flowing work garment." The Greek is *gumnos*, which means "naked," but that can also mean "scantily clothed," so it could mean either.

When the fishermen land the boat, there is a charcoal fire with fish and bread cooking. Jesus tells them to bring some of the fish in the net. They pull the net ashore and count the fish—153! Jesus invites them to come and have breakfast. No one asks who Jesus is, for they know he is the risen living Lord. Jesus then serves them bread and fish.

…

The writer states nothing about symbolism in the number of fish, but interpreters knowing the significance of "signs" in John's gospel have tried to discover some imagery in it. For example,

- *Cyril of Alexandria said that 100 represents the fullness of Gentile inclusion in the church, 50 represents the remnant of Israel that will be gathered in, and 3 represents the Trinity.*
- *Augustine said that there are 10 commandments and 7 gifts of the Spirit, and 153 is the sum of all numbers 1-17, so the number of fish represents all who will come to God by Law and by Grace.*
- *Jerome said there are a total of 153 species of fish, so the fish in the net represent the total of all people who will be gathered into the net of God's grace.*
- *Some interpreters have seen in this a symbolic reference to the supper in the upper room on the night before the Crucifixion.*

…

JESUS AND SIMON PETER
(21:15-17)

After breakfast Jesus speaks with Peter. Three times Jesus asks if Peter loves him. Three times Peter answers that he does. To each reply Jesus assigns a task of service: "feed/tend my lambs/sheep." Peter is "grieved" that Jesus asks the question a third time.

Twice Jesus asks Peter "Do you love (*agape*) me?" Twice Peter answers, "You know I love (*phileo*) you." The third time Jesus asks, "Do you love (*phileo*) me?" Peter, grieved because of the third questioning, still says, "You know that I love (*phileo*) you."

There is a fundamental difference in the basic meanings of *agape* and *phileo*. *Agape* refers to esteem—to hold a person in high regard for their status, position, or worth.[5] *Phileo* refers more to a spontaneous, emotional reaction—to like, to want to be friends with.[6]

...

This beautiful passage is often called the restoration of Peter. I prefer to describe it as the reconciliation with Peter. It is impossible not to see in the threefold question-and-answer structure of the conversation a reference to the threefold denial by Peter of his relationship to Jesus during the night of the betrayal, arrest, and trial. Because of Peter's denial, the personal relationship between Peter and Jesus has been damaged. Peter is shamed, saddened, and guilt-ridden by what he has done. It is deep enough a hurt to leave him feeling estranged from Jesus. What he needs is to feel forgiven and to be reconciled.

The agape/phileo *distinction is important in human relations, but for both the focus of "love" is the point.*

- Agape *means the focus of my love is on you because you are esteemed of great worth. I want what you want because I am convinced of its worth, as in prayer for the will of God to be done.*
- Agape, *as God's love for us, focuses on us. God loves us because of what he wants to do for us, not for what we can "add" for him. Agape can well be translated "care for," as in I love/ care for you because I value you so highly that I want only the best for you.*
- Phileo *means the focus of my love for you is about what it means for me, as in I like you, I find it pleasant to share life with you, I wish to have you as a friend.*
- Phileo *can well be translated "like," as in I love/like you because we are enough alike to enjoy being friends.*

Agape *and* phileo *are described as synonyms, but the focal direction of "love" in human relationships has vital effect on the quality of the relationships.*

Jesus asks Peter if his love is agape. *Does Peter esteem Jesus highly enough to give him the loyalty he deserves as Lord and Christ? Peter does not seem able to affirm that great esteem, that kind of love. Psychologically, Peter may not have yet become able to believe one like himself who has proven disloyal can possibly measure up to that standard. What he can and does say is, "Lord, I am your friend." The same question and answer are repeated a second time. The third time Jesus asks, "Simon, are you really my friend?"*

Simon is grieved (heartbroken, Greek: elupethe = *to be in distress, to grieve) that Jesus asks him the third time about his devotion. In other words, his self-loathing for having denied Jesus three times is so great that a third question hits him hard. The most he is able to say is still, "Lord, you know everything, you know I am your friend."*

The response Jesus makes each time to Peter's answer is an affirming assignment, as much as to say to Peter, "You are one of mine; feed my lambs/tend my sheep/feed my sheep." The rift of Peter's denial is over and done. Jesus affirms to Peter that he is still to be that central leader, the Rock.

...

WORDS OF COUNSEL
(21:18-19)

Jesus speaks words of counsel to Peter, which should instruct all of us. The Gospels record that Peter is the first to speak, boldest to promise, most extravagant with claims of loyalty. He proves that he has "clay feet." Jesus describes Peter as an outspoken, self-confident, "dress yourself and go where you please" sort of person. Jesus warns him that it will not always be so, "when you are old." It is as if to say to Peter, "A little humility on your part will be fitting." His last word to Peter, however, is like his first. At their first meeting Jesus said, "Follow me and I will make you become fishers of men" (Mark 1:17). "You are Cephas (a rock)" (John 1:42). Here, at this moment of reconciliation, Jesus says to Peter again, "Follow me."

Verse 19 is an interpretation by the author of John. He writes that "stretching out his hands" is to show "by what death he (Peter) would die." The statement is placed in parentheses in the Revised Standard Version. It seems likely this writer may well have known the tradition that Peter was crucified as a martyr in Rome some three decades before this gospel was written.

WHAT ABOUT JOHN?
(21:20-23)

Following the words of counsel from Jesus to Peter, a conversation ensues between the two about the destiny of "the disciple whom Jesus loved" (assumed to be John). Peter asks, "What about him?" Jesus in effect says to Peter, "His future and destiny are not a matter of your concern. Your concern should focus on yourself and my calling to you to follow me." Rumors tend to spring to life with the very least of grounds, or with no grounds at all. The "saying spread that John would not die." The writer corrects that unfounded rumor.

THE WRITER'S ASSERTION
(21:24-25)

The author of John then places a second ending to this gospel (see above 20:30-31). The writer declares himself to be, for the document, both the writer of it and a witness to the truthfulness of it. He also affirms the limitation of what he has written. What Jesus has done is so awesomely universal that the totality of it simply cannot be put into written documents.

...

What Jesus has done in incarnation, the Holy Spirit will continue to do in perpetuity as Emmanuel/Paraclete, God with us, forever (see John 14:15-18).

...

NOTES

[1] Wilbert F. Howard, "The Gospel According to St. John, Exegesis," *The Interpreter's Bible, vol. 8,* (New York: Abingdon Press, 1952), 797-798.

[2] Reinhold Seeberg, *Text-book of the History of Doctrines, pt. 1,* (Grand Rapids: Baker Book House,1954), 61.

[3] Ibid., *Doctrines,* 319.

[4] "Absolution," *Catholic Encyclopedia Online* (web search).

[5] G. Abbott-Smith, *A Manuel Greek Lexicon of the New Testament,* (Edinburgh: T&T Clark, 1950), 3-4.

[6] Ibid., *Lexicon,* 469.

www.ingramcontent.com/pod-product-compliance
Lightning Source LLC
Chambersburg PA
CBHW071007160426
43193CB00012B/1951